Past-into-Present Series

TOWNS

Charles Whynne-Hammond

B.T. BATSFORD LTD, London

ISBN 0 7134 3066 4

Printed by The Anchor Press, Tiptree, Essex
for the Publishers B. T. Batsford Ltd,
4 Fitzhardinge Street London W1H 0AH

Ackowledgment

The Author and Publishers would like to thank the following for their kind permission to reproduce copyright illustrations: the National Museum of Wales for fig 4; the Bodleian Library, Oxford, for fig 6; A.F. Kersting for figs 8, 9, 43, 51; the Bibliothèque Royale, Bruxelles, for fig 10; the Raymond Mander and Joe Mitchenson Theatre Collection for fig 12; the Mansell Collection for fig 31; the Science Museum, London, for figs 36, 50; Edwin Smith for fig 37; Edinburgh Libraries for fig 38; the National Coal Board for fig 41; London Transport for figs 49, 61; Aerofilms for figs 52, 53; the Cumbernauld Development Corporation for fig 57; Bellwood Photography Ltd, Sheffield, for fig 59; Popperfoto for figs 60, 65; *Coventry Evening Telegraph* for fig 62; and Associated Newspapers Ltd for fig 63. The other pictures appearing in this book are the property of the Publishers.

Contents

List of Illustrations

Chapter 1
The First Towns

The Earliest Settlements

No-one really knows when the first towns were developed or who built them. This is because there is almost no evidence: very few written accounts survive and ancient sites rarely give archaeologists a chance for detailed excavation. All we do know is that towns first appeared very early on indeed in the history of civilization.

The earliest settlements were probably no more than small groups of huts whose inhabitants depended entirely on farming for their livelihood. In such places, early man found friendship in times of peace, help in times of hardship and protection in times of war. He supplied his own food, made his own clothes, weapons and tools, and cared little for the outside world.

However, with the passage of time, the character of these communities changed. Rather than do everything themselves, people began to specialize in doing what they were good at, and barter for the other goods they needed. For example, a man who made pots would find it easier to trade his pots with a farmer in exchange for food rather than spend part of his time farming. Similarly, the farmer might prefer to swap his grain for tools rather than make them himself. In this way industries and trade developed. Gradually settlements began to house more craftsmen and merchants than farmers or labourers, and thus became more detached from agriculture. Once this happened, however partially, the settlements ceased to be villages and became towns.

Probably towns of this kind first developed in south-east Asia before 5,500 BC when other parts of the world were still in the Stone Age. Soon after, they appeared in other regions: in Mesopotamia, the Middle East and China, and possibly even in America although, as yet, we have no definite evidence of this. Often they were located on important trading routes which further encouraged trade and urban development. Babylon, for example, grew up in Mesopotamia on a great overland trade route across Asia. By 3,500 BC it had become the largest city in the East, with a flourishing trade in dyes, cloth, gold and silver, jewellery and spices, and a population of 80,000 people.

As industry and trade developed, these early settlements grew rich and their inhabitants became cultured and wealthy. Babylon, with its palaces, hanging

6 gardens and temples, was not the only town built on a grand scale. Such urban opulence was common in the ancient world. In Egypt the remains of Tel-el-Amarna, which was built about 1640 BC, still give archaeologists today a good idea of what the original town looked like all those centuries ago. There was a market place in the centre, running down to the River Nile; magnificent temples to the sun god, Aten; three palaces for the king (the Pharaoh Akhnaten); a 30-roomed house for the king's chief minister; numerous other houses; and shops for blacksmiths, barbers, weavers, armourers, dyers and sandal makers.

By 2,000 BC town building had reached the eastern Mediterranean. It was at about this time that the famous city of Troy was first founded. Here was the meeting place of the great shipping routes between Europe and Asia, and Troy soon became the most important port for both continents.

The rise of the Greek civilization led inevitably to the spread of towns. By the tenth century BC, Greece was a country of regional capitals, each one the major commercial, political and social centre for the surrounding area. The Greek 'polis' — or regional capital — is of particular significance in the history of towns since it was here that the first real town planning took place. Henceforth, many towns did not merely grow out irregularly from their original centres but were planned as definite urban units. The ancient remains at Athens still show the effects of such planning: straight roads crossing each other at right angles, large square public buildings, well laid-out gardens and parks and, in the centre, the acropolis — the great religious and commercial focus of town life.

Greek colonization meant the building of towns throughout the Mediterranean. By the second century BC, towns existed as far west as Spain and as far north as the Alps. But it was to take the Romans, and the spread of their empire, to bring towns to Britain.

1 (*Above right*) A reconstruction showing a primitive settlement. From earliest times the well was the centre of village life.

2 (*Right*) Athens. Even today the Acropolis and ancient Greek remains dominate the city.

8

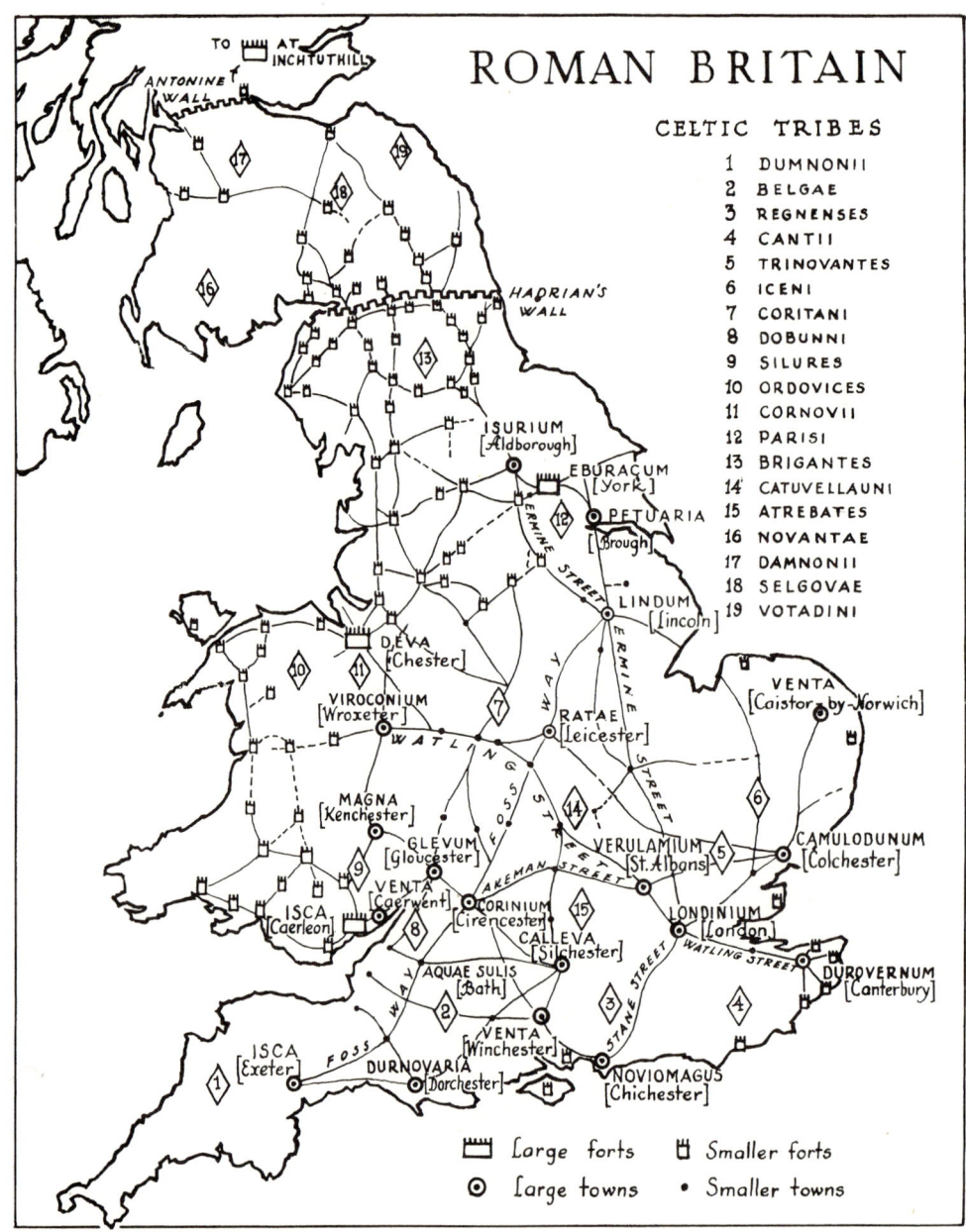

ROMAN BRITAIN

CELTIC TRIBES

1 DUMNONII
2 BELGAE
3 REGNENSES
4 CANTII
5 TRINOVANTES
6 ICENI
7 CORITANI
8 DOBUNNI
9 SILURES
10 ORDOVICES
11 CORNOVII
12 PARISI
13 BRIGANTES
14 CATUVELLAUNI
15 ATREBATES
16 NOVANTAE
17 DAMNONII
18 SELGOVAE
19 VOTADINI

TO 🏰 AT INCHTUTHILL
ANTONINE WALL
HADRIAN'S WALL
ISURIUM [Aldborough]
EBURACUM [York]
PETUARIA [Brough]
LINDUM [Lincoln]
DEVA [Chester]
VIROCONIUM [Wroxeter]
RATAE [Leicester]
VENTA [Caistor by Norwich]
ERMINE STREET
WATLING STREET
MAGNA [Kenchester]
GLEVUM [Gloucester]
VERULAMIUM [St. Albans]
CAMULODUNUM [Colchester]
FOSS STREET
AKEMAN STREET
VENTA [Caerwent]
CORINIUM [Cirencester]
LONDINIUM [London]
ISCA [Caerleon]
CALLEVA [Silchester]
WATLING STREET
AQUAE SULIS [Bath]
DUROVERNUM [Canterbury]
STANE STREET
ISCA [Exeter]
DURNOVARIA [Dorchester]
VENTA [Winchester]
NOVIOMAGUS [Chichester]
FOSS

🏰 Large forts   🏰 Smaller forts
⊙ Large towns   • Smaller towns

3 The roads and settlements of Roman Britain. Many of the Celtic tribes shown here quickly became 'Romanized'.

'The Britons call it a town when they have occupied woods and fortified them with a rampart and a ditch.' So wrote Julius Caesar just over 2,000 years ago when he led the first Roman invasion of this country. At that time Britain was a place of wild moorlands, dense forests and extensive marshes. There were no towns as we know them. The inhabitants — mostly Celtic peoples who came originally from central Europe — lived by tilling the poor soils for grain and using the rough pastures for rearing cattle and sheep. The only settlements were tiny agricultural villages. Towns as commercial and administrative centres simply did not exist.

The Romans changed all this. During the centuries after AD 43, the year of their second invasion, Britain was given a network of roads, a set of military camps and fortresses, many miles of defensive walls and, most important of all, a number of towns. 'To make a town of the whole world' was, to the Romans, the chief aim of empire. To this end, therefore, Roman organization, money and manpower was deployed in massive building schemes all over the country, involving either the development of existing tribal villages or the creation of entirely new settlements.

Fortunately both archaeological and literary evidence has given us a fairly good idea of what these Roman towns were like. Their most marked feature was their layout. Set within defensive stone walls, often as much as 6 metres high, each town was laid out in a 'chessboard' pattern with the streets crossing each other at right angles and the rectangular areas between being used for buildings or open spaces. The roads themselves were generally paved with flat, interlocking stone slabs, and usually had gutters on either side to allow for drainage. Only the very minor streets were left unpaved, although, even on these, the Romans sometimes used a mixture of sand and gravel to stop the surface from becoming too muddy.

The public buildings were the largest and by far the most advanced feature of a Roman town. Built of marble, granite, bricks and even concrete, they rose sometimes to well over 25 metres and completely dominated the skyline. In the middle stood the 'forum', or market place. This was usually decorated with statues, monuments and drinking fountains, and acted as the main commercial and social centre. Next to this was the 'basilica', the main administrative building. This was rather like our modern town hall and included a number of small rooms, probably for the use of local governors, together with some larger rooms which might be used for banquets and similar social functions. Other public buildings found in most Roman towns include baths, theatres and circuses. You can find out what these looked like from their remains. The Roman baths at Bath and the amphitheatre at Verulamium (St Albans) are both well worth a visit.

Like the public buildings, the private buildings in Roman towns were laid out in squares. Unfortunately, however, they were not as advanced in their construction. The lodging houses, taverns, shops and houses were usually made

10 only of timber, wattle and daub, or even just baked mud. Some were extremely humble. At Calleva Atrebatum (Silchester) for example, archaeologists have found evidence of tiny hut dwellings, each with only one or two rooms, no windows, and with bare earthen floors.

The shops were an interesting feature in these towns. They tended to be long and narrow and were usually packed closely together along the main streets. Each one had an open front, with a counter facing the pavement, which could be covered by wooden shutters at closing time. A large back room was used as a workshop or store-room, and it was here that the shopkeeper would be making or mending his wares while his wife and children served customers. Even young children, no more than four or five years old, would help out in the shop. A short flight of steps led from the back room to a couple of rooms upstairs, above the shop, where the shopkeeper and his family slept.

The Romans were a civilized people, priding themselves on their cleanliness, and their expert engineering enabled them to supply their towns with a continuous flow of fresh water. This was an expensive operation, and often meant the complicated construction of underground channels and pipes, the digging of long canals or the building of high aqueducts.

However, they did not take the same care over drainage and the disposal of sewage. Lindum (Lincoln) was the exception: here there was an elaborate network of outflow channels and drains, all equipped with manholes and volume controls. Other towns were not as lucky. A central midden would normally be provided onto which the inhabitants could empty their buckets of waste and slops. If some people were lazy, or if the cesspit were a long way off, the slop buckets would simply be emptied out of the window into the street below. One cannot help feeling sorry for the unfortunate passers-by!

What wonderful places these towns must have seemed to the visiting Celt. All round him were milling crowds: wealthy magistrates in white woollen togas with purple edging, and ladies in their fine silks and cottons and their hair piled high with ringlets and jewels. Even many of his own people had been 'Romanized' and were dressed fairly well: colourful tunics, with thick cloaks and sandals on their feet. And what sights! Great four-wheeled carts, or 'roedas', loaded down with goods, fast two-wheeled chariots driven by rich young men, and, every now and then, a 'lectica' or sedan-chair carried along by two servants with their mistress inside. How he would gaze in wonder at the decorated shops: red pottery, ornaments, tools and weapons, brooches made of tin, bronze or silver, and jewellery all laid out on the counters. And there, through the glass windows, was the dim gleam of light from candles and oil lamps, and the burning charcoal cinders in the open fires. And the noise! Town criers shouting the news of recent victories in the Empire; announcements of the coming entertainments at the amphitheatre, and, in the distance, the loud bargaining of the buying and selling of slaves — poor wretches from the conquered lands of northern Europe brought to this country to serve in bondage for the rest of their lives. These towns were indeed strange and exciting places.

By modern standards they were not very large. Most Roman towns covered less than 100 hectares, and had a population of about 4,000 people. This would make them roughly the size of a large village today. Nevertheless they were very successful, both as centres of social and commercial activity and as important administrative capitals. As early as AD 60 London was described by Tacitus, the Roman historian, as the chief residence of merchants and a flourishing trade centre. By the third century it was not only the most important town in Britain, but was also one of the largest trading centres north of the Alps.

Unlike any previous settlements in Britain, Roman towns were largely independent of agriculture. Though they held weekly markets where farm produce could be bought and sold, their wealth was based on industry and trade. Pottery, utensils, tiles and bricks, leather goods and textiles became the common artefacts of urban life, and were sold widely throughout Britain and Europe. These Roman towns formed the first link in a chain of urban development which has stretched almost unbroken to the present day.

4 Venta Silurum, now Caerwent in Monmouthshire. Notice the farmland outside the town walls.

5 A reconstruction of a busy street scene in Roman Britain.

The Dark Ages

In AD 410 the last of the Roman armies departed from Britain, and the Celts were left to run their own affairs. For a while they managed fairly well; the Roman towns were kept in good repair and, in general, urban life continued much as before. But this situation did not last for long. Gradually tribes from northern Europe came to our shores, at first only to raid the land and destroy the villages, but later to settle permanently. And as these new invaders moved across the country so the Celts fled westwards to seek safety in the hills. Within a mere century of the departure of the Romans, the Celts had settled in Scotland, Ireland, Wales and Cornwall, and England had become the land of the Anglo-Saxons.

Unlike the Romans, the Saxons were agriculturalists, who lived mainly on farming and had little need for large urban centres. Indeed, when they came to this country, they hardly knew what real towns were. According to contemporary writers, they believed the large Roman buildings were either the work of giants or places haunted by evil spirits. Thus, under the Saxons, many Roman towns fell into decay. Houses became derelict and roads degenerated into grassy tracks, often entirely obliterated by vegetation.

However, it would be wrong to think that towns disappeared altogether. Some did survive as local trading centres for groups of merchants and craftsmen, some Celtic, some foreign, who did their best to keep the buildings in reasonable repair. In the seventh century, for example, we are told that when St Cuthbert visited Carlisle, the Roman fountain there was still in working order. At about the same time, Bede, a monk from Jarrow, wrote that London was 'the metropolis of the East Saxons . . . a market place of many people coming by land and sea'. Yet it was to be many centuries before Britain once again became a land of towns.

As an agricultural race the Saxons were eager to extend the area under cultivation in Britain. They cut down forests and drained marshes in order to grow more crops and rear more animals. With this extension of agriculture a large number of new settlements grew up, each one the centre of local farming activity. Some of these were on or near old Roman sites and were given names like 'chester' from the Latin *castra* meaning a camp. Others developed around the houses of tribal leaders and had names ending in 'wich', from the Saxon word *wic* meaning a country house. Yet others grew as defensive settlements and became 'burhs', from which we derive the modern town names ending in 'bury' and 'borough'.

Gradually many of these villages started to grow in size and importance. Agriculture became more prosperous; the population of the country rose, and industries and crafts developed to supply the needs of the village communities. This in turn led to an increase in trade, not just between different settlements but between England and Europe. The result of all this was inevitable. Villages expanded and became market centres for the surrounding area. In time they took on newer functions still, either acting as administrative capitals or becoming religious centres grouped around the new monasteries built by Christian missionaries. As early as the sixth century, for instance, records show that Canterbury had already been rebuilt from the old Roman remains and had become the capital and seat of the Kentish kings.

The coming of the Vikings and Danes, who invaded and settled in eastern England during the eighth and ninth centuries, gave further encouragement to the growth of towns. These Scandinavian people were by nature town dwellers and traders, and the area that fell under their rule — known as the Danelaw — quickly became a region of large commercial and political centres. By AD 800 the 'Five Boroughs' (Derby, Stamford, Nottingham, Leicester and Lincoln) had grown into major Danish towns with populations of about 6,000.

In both Danish and Saxon England towns grew in response to changing economic conditions. They were not planned, like Roman towns, but grew up as a jumble of irregular, narrow streets and rough timber houses. Many places,

14 like Canterbury, had laws stipulating the space to be left between buildings, but these laws had little effect. Roads and houses were crowded, light and open space were restricted, and good sanitation was almost non-existent.

Nevertheless, the two centuries preceding the Norman Conquest of 1066 saw the greatest advance in town life since the Romans. The everyday running of each town was put into the hands of a group of inhabitants who banded together into 'guilds'. These were the forerunners of our modern town councils. Law and order were enforced by courts which were set up under full-time judges and had juries of twelve men drawn from the 'ceorls' or freemen of the borough. The old custom of bartering for goods died out, and money was now accepted as the usual form of payment. As a result, the right to mint coins — which was considered a great honour — became another sign of a town's growing importance.

By the eleventh century, England was once more a land of towns. Urban populations of over 5,000 were common, and it was usual for the larger ports to have trading links as far away as Germany and Italy. London in particular grew into a thriving commercial centre with a strong system of local government.

The foundations of modern town life had been laid.

6 This early medieval manuscript shows the king and his councillors sheltering in a burh.

Chapter 2
The Middle Ages

Castle and Church

By the time William the Conqueror invaded Britain in 1066, most of the settlements we know as towns today were already in existence. Apart from the numerous hamlets and villages there were over 100 Saxon communities large enough to be called boroughs. Each of these had the wealth and functions that usually went with the title: a mint, a busy trade, shops and industries, and a form of local government. In 1086, exactly 20 years after the Norman invasion, a detailed survey, called the Domesday Book, was compiled for the whole of England. Already this described 16 boroughs as 'cities' because of their great power and prestige. And during the next 500 years English towns continued to grow with ever greater momentum.

In order to maintain their power and keep the Saxons under control, the Normans built numerous castles up and down the country. Some of these were made of wood, but many were massive stone constructions the like of which had never been known before in Britain. They towered over the fields and dominated the countryside for miles around. The Saxons could not overcome this defensive system and were forced to accept the Norman barons as their overlords. In some places, they even managed to benefit from the castles by building their houses outside the walls and supplying the needs of the soldiers for food, clothing and entertainment. Newcastle-upon-Tyne, Ludlow and Pembroke all developed in this way.

But the Normans did not only build castles. Their masons and builders were also skilled at erecting the churches, cathedrals and monasteries which formed such an integral part of the Norman way of life. At the end of the Saxon period there were just 35 monasteries in England; by the end of the twelfth century, a little over 100 years later, there were four times this number. Just as the civic buildings — the forum and basilica — had formed the core of every Roman town, so in medieval times even the smallest village depended on its church or monastery. As the years passed, these religious houses grew in power and wealth, and their influence extended to every man, woman and child in the country. It was in the monasteries and nunneries that the sick were tended, travellers found rest and scholarship blossomed. Almost all the great towns that we know today — London, York, Canterbury, Durham, Winchester and many, many more — rose to prominence around their religious core.

16   The Wool Trade

Between 1066 and the start of Queen Elizabeth I's reign in 1558, various economic and social forces were at work altering Britain's landscape and causing a further increase in town building and town wealth.

Perhaps the most fundamental developments of all were the changes in farming and trade. Once the Normans had restored peace to the land, British agriculture again prospered. But this time its prosperity was not based solely on crops as it had been during the Dark Ages. Wool was soon to be the farmers' most important source of income. English wool was generally recognized as the best in the world, and foreign merchants were willing to pay very high prices for it. Gradually the open fields and strips of the Saxons were enclosed for the grazing of sheep, especially in areas like the Pennines, the Midland plain, the West Country and East Anglia where local conditions made it particularly profitable.

The effects of this change-over to sheep grazing were far-reaching indeed. The wool was exported to the weavers of Flanders, North Germany, Italy and France, and, in time, made up the principal part of England's trade. All round the coast old seaports sprang into life and new ones emerged; places like Southampton, Boston, Sandwich, Hull and Bristol suddenly expanded and became extremely wealthy. Other exports also led to the growth of these towns. A book produced in Bruges, Belgium, in about 1200 tells us that 'from England come wool, hides, lead, tin, coal and cheese'. As the country became richer so more goods were imported, especially luxuries like jewellery, spices, ivory and silk.

But it was not only the coastal towns which felt the effects of sheep farming. Inland the new type of agriculture meant that less farm-workers were needed. After all, a single shepherd could tend a whole flock of sheep. Small tenant farmers and labourers were thus turned off the land because there was no work for them to do. These luckless people had little choice but to move to the towns, where there was at least some hope of employment in a shop or workroom. This movement of population from countryside to town naturally led to further urban growth.

By the fourteenth century England's own cloth trade had begun to flourish. For a variety of political, religious and economic reasons, hundreds of European weavers were forced to leave their homeland. Many came to settle in this country where they continued their work, and towns like Winchester, Salisbury, Exeter and Colchester soon became centres of a thriving cloth industry. Thus it was that a rich wool trade was transformed into an equally rich cloth trade, and coastal and inland towns alike reaped the benefit.

The immense wealth which resulted from this meant that town buildings could be erected on a much grander scale. Everywhere great churches were being built, and vast amounts of money were poured into new construction schemes. A notable advance in this respect was the revival, however limited, of town-planning. Where towns were rebuilt, either by choice or of necessity, the old Roman 'chessboard' pattern was used, with intersecting streets and rectangular housing blocks between. As early as 1220, Richard Poore, Bishop of Salisbury, left his windswept, cramped, hilltop town and laid out a completely new one on his own meadows by the River Avon. The town he left became known as Old Sarum and soon disappeared, while his new town became New Sarum, or Salisbury, and grew to great importance. Similarly, in 1283, Edward I gave permission for a new town to be built at Winchelsea in Sussex after the original had been swept away by the sea. This became New Winchelsea and, like Salisbury, followed a very exact and formal grid pattern.

Such examples of town-planning were, however, only too few and far between. On the whole, medieval towns remained very unhealthy places. Streets were dark and narrow, houses were shabbily built of wood and plaster and stood close together, leaving no room for ventilation, and people still dumped their refuse in the public thoroughfares. The channel or gutter which ran down the middle of most streets was nothing more than an open sewer, and on hot days the stench was frightful. These conditions encouraged the spread of disease, particularly the plague. The worst outbreak came in the middle of the fourteenth century, when the Black Death killed one million people, about a third of Britain's total population.

7 Oxford. The regular layout of this university town was established in early medieval times.

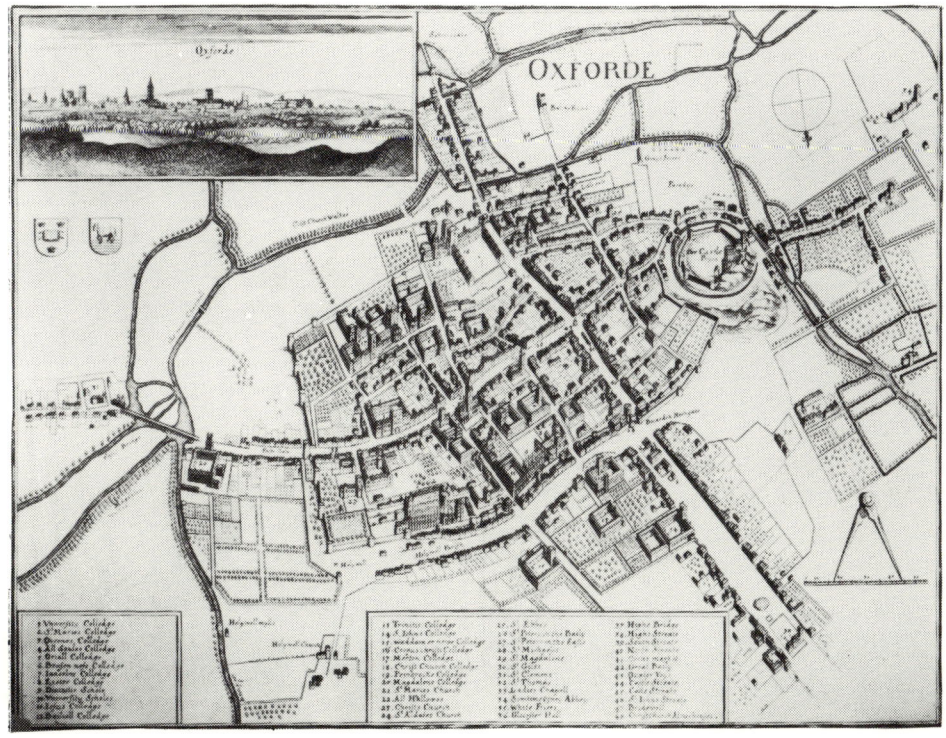

8 Castle Hedingham in Essex: a typical Norman castle.

9 Huish Episcopi Church, Somerset: built with the profits from the wool trade.

10 A town receiving its municipal charter.

Despite such obvious disadvantages to town life, Britain's urban population continued to increase and towns grew steadily larger and more numerous. As the Middle Ages wore on, a number of these towns began to dominate the rest. They developed their own special functions and rivalled each other in economic power and social prestige. Oxford, for instance, had its university and Norwich its silverware. London, above all, became the acknowledged capital. Even as early as the twelfth century it was renowned for its schools, its law courts, its charities and its water supply. William FitzStephen's description of London during the reign of Henry II (1154-89) tells us a great deal:

> Among the noble and celebrated cities of the world that of London, the capital of the kingdom of the English, is one which extends its glory farther than all the others and sends its wealth and merchandise more widely into distant lands . . . I do not think there is a city with a better record for church-going, doing honour to God's ordinances, keeping feast-days, giving alms and hospitality to strangers, confirming betrothals, contracting marriages, celebrating weddings, providing feasts, entertaining guests and also, it may be added, in care for funerals and for the burial of the dead. The only plagues of London are the immoderate drinking of fools and the frequency of fires.

York, a religious centre and the main cloth town of northern England, was the second largest city in Britain and, at times, even seemed to lay claim to its right as the English capital. Bristol was the third largest, closely followed by numerous other towns including Winchester, Lincoln, Norwich, Canterbury and Boston.

The development of the wool industry gave new impetus to town expansion. This in its turn led to a stronger system of local government and town organization. All this, plus a tremendous increase in the importance of charters, guilds, markets and fairs, created a whole new concept of town life.

Charters
In many ways the Normans were far more used to town life than the Saxons. There had been large towns in Normandy, as well as in the rest of France, for many centuries, and a prosperous trade had long made the Normans a rich and powerful race. Now, under the new conquerors, town life in England became more popular. In particular, a stronger system of local government gave the towns greater independence and the ability to cope with their growing importance.

The most important man in each town was the mayor. He would preside over the meetings of the townsmen, sit as a magistrate in the court, and generally act as the king's representative in the running of the town. His chief helpers would include the 'jurats' or councillors, the Town Clerk, who kept a record of everything that happened, and the Common Serjeant. The task of the Common Serjeant was to keep 'watch and ward' over the town — rather like the police force today. He would choose a number of men, perhaps 15, and together they would patrol the streets at night, watch out for fires, supervise the market and make sure that honest trading was maintained, and keep an eye on any strangers who might be staying in town.

Although these officials were the forerunners of our modern town councils, they enjoyed far greater powers. Unlike today, towns then were self-governing almost to the point of being independent states. Each town had its own bye-laws or ordinances which were strictly enforced by the authorities. These ordinances were usually sensible laws, determined by the particular needs of the community. For example, housewives were often not allowed to wash clothes in the local river because that was the only supply of fresh water for cooking and brewing. Similarly, in many towns, animals were forbidden to wander in or foul the streets, and some towns banned the use of carts with iron-rimmed wheels because they would break up the road surfaces.

Before a town could become self-governing, however, it had to have a charter. These charters were granted by the Norman kings to towns which they considered were large enough or wealthy enough to run their own affairs. Each charter set down the rights and privileges of the townsmen, allowed for the election of a council, and often gave permission for the shopkeepers and merchants to hold a weekly market. The following is a typical charter; it was given to the city of Gloucester by Henry II in the twelfth century:

Henry, king of the English and duke of the Normans, count of the Angevins, to all archbishops, bishops, abbots, earls, barons, justices, sheriffs and to all his liegemen of the whole of England, both French and English, greeting. Know that I have granted and confirmed to my burgesses of Gloucester the same customs and liberties throughout all my land in respect of toll and all other things, as well as ever the citizens of London and Winchester had them in the time of King Henry, my grandfather. Wherefore I will, and firmly order, that my aforesaid burgesses shall have all those liberties, and free customs and full quittances, and that no one in respect of these shall cause them injury, or loss, or molestation.

But the Norman kings did not grant a charter for nothing. The town so endowed had either to pay a large sum of money into the Treasury or provide a particular service. This was how the 'cinque ports' developed. They were the five most important towns on the south-east coast of England — Hastings, Romney, Hythe, Dover and Sandwich — and their name comes from the French word *cinq* meaning five. Later two more towns were added to the list — Winchelsea and Rye. The service these towns were to provide for the king was made only too clear in the charter given to them by Edward I:

At each time that the king passeth over the seas, the ports ought to rig up
fifty-and-seven ships (whereof every one to have twenty armed soldiers) and
to maintain them at their own costs, for the space of fifteen days together.

Guilds

Once a charter had been granted a town was free to grow and prosper without
much interference from the king. The most significant feature of trade and
industry in each town was the guild, an association of people involved in the
same line of business. The guilds had come into existence under the Saxons but
now, with the emergence of charters and civic independence, they expanded
and became very much more important.

There were two types of guilds in medieval England: merchant guilds
formed by groups of traders and people dealing in commerce, and craft guilds
set up by craftsmen and their workers. In the former category were guilds
specializing in products such as wool, leather and wine, while the latter
included guilds for tailors, barbers, bakers and so on.

In general, however, both types of guild shared the same basic aims. They
wished to keep all business in their own hands, to limit the numbers entering
their profession, and to maintain high standards of workmanship. They also
looked after the running of markets, saw that honest trading was kept by
checking the weights, measures and quality of all goods sold, and made sure
that hours of work and conditions of employment remained fair. On top of all
this they did a great deal of charitable work. In return for the high membership
fees they looked after the general well-being of their members. They gave help
to those who fell ill, provided for widows and orphans of those who had died,
and sometimes even paid for the building of churches and hospitals.

On holy days like Whitsun and the feast of Corpus Christi they also provided
entertainment for the townsfolk. This usually took the form of pageants,
miracle or mystery plays, which were loosely based on biblical stories and
combined both comedy and drama with songs, poetry and dances. The
costumes used in these early plays were often very colourful, and masks,
dragons' heads and 'devils' became common features.

The craft guilds, in particular, did much to encourage improvements in
standards of workmanship. The master-craftsmen took on apprentices who
normally served for a period of seven years during which they lived with their
employers. In time apprentices would become journeymen, or daytime
workmen, and take over some of their masters' tasks. Keen and conscientious
journeymen might eventually become masters themselves and take on their
own apprentices. All masters, journeymen and apprentices in the same trade
belonged to the same guild. Each guild organized training schemes and made
sure that their journeymen and apprentices led respectable lives. In fact, some
guild rules were extremely strict. At Coventry, for example, the journeymen
were forbidden to frequent inns on weekdays:

as it is daylye seen that they whiche be of the pooreste sorte doo sytte all daye in the alehouse drynkynge and playnge at the cardes and tables and spende all that they can gett prodigally upon themselfes to the highe displeasure of God and theyre owne ympovershynge, whereas if it were spente at home in theyre owne houses theyre wiffes and childerne shulde have parte therof.

With a strong internal organization and a great deal of freedom, guilds were soon able to control all the commercial life of a town. In some places they became so powerful that they even gained control of the political and social administration of the town. When this happened the guildhall became the centre of a town's government and our modern town hall was born.

11 (*Left*) Building a house. Each workman in this medieval picture would have belonged to a craft guild.

12 (*Right*) A mystery play being performed in the streets of Coventry.

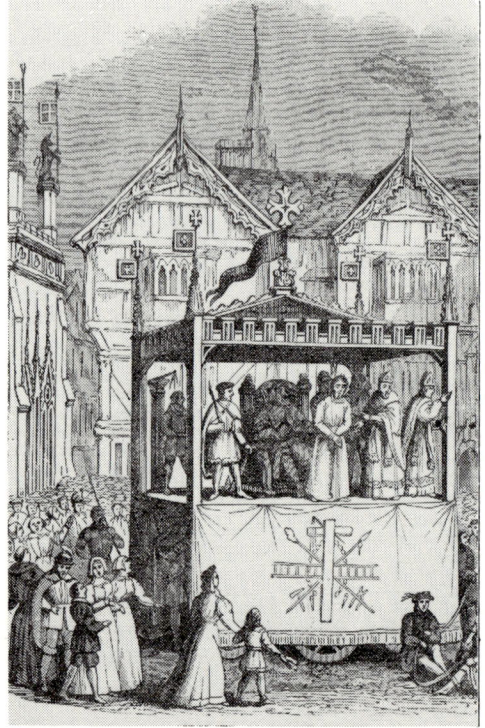

One of the most valuable sources of income for many towns was their market. However, before organizing a regular market, a town had to obtain royal permission. This was either included in the charter or was made by a separate grant from the king. In both cases the town had to pay dearly for the privilege, or rather the guilds had to, since it was usually the guilds which organized the markets and reaped the benefits. Once permission had been given, a town could prosper since markets brought in a great deal of money. They also gave towns influence over their surrounding areas and increased their prestige as commercial centres. It is little wonder that townspeople took great pride in their markets and showed open hostility to any others nearby which were likely to take away some of their custom.

Markets were usually held once a week either in a market place or along the narrow streets. Market day was a great local event. Country people came from miles around with their carts and sacks to sell their farm produce on the stones: corn, cheese, meat, wool and so on. The townsfolk, likewise, set up stalls and sold their goods: cloth, leather, shoes, pottery and tools. Everywhere there was the general confusion of a great social gathering. People gossiped and exchanged news, ate and drank at the open food stalls and made merry with their friends and families. In the sixteenth century one poet described a market scene like this:

> This Barnet is a place of great resort
> And commonly upon the market days
> Here all the country gentlemen appoint
> A friendly meeting; some about affairs
> Of consequence and profit — bargain, sale
> And to confer with chapmen: some for pleasure,
> To match their horses, wager in their dogs
> Or try their hawks: some to no other end
> But only meet good company, discourse,
> Dine, drink and spend their money.

In these markets, trades tended to be grouped together, and different streets became the centres for different types of shops and stalls. There was usually a Cornmarket for grain, a Butterwalk for dairy produce and a Meatmarket or Shambles for butchers. Sometimes the groups of stalls were quite extensive. In Norwich market, for example, records for 1397 show there were as many as 40 butchers' stalls together, 45 fishmongers' and 28 poulterers'. With this arrangement markets certainly gave customers a wide choice of quality and prices.

The mayors, jurats, common serjeants and guild officials between them checked to make sure that fair trading in the market was maintained. This was no easy matter since most stallholders were likely to try and make a dishonest

24 profit should the opportunity arise. Practices such as giving short weight, using false coins and selling poor quality goods were widespread. Bakers, butchers and brewers were especially liable to such illegal dealings since, in their trades, cheating customers was relatively easy. A dishonest baker could be fined 21 pence for a first and second offence, but on the third occasion his oven might be destroyed. The pillory was another common punishment, and traders who sold bad meat or fish were sometimes tied down and had the stinking flesh burned under their noses. Overcharging was equally common and just as disliked by the town officials. In 1382 a London fishmonger named Thomas Welford was compelled by the authorities to reduce the price of his herrings since they were considered to be not of sufficiently high quality. He was forced to sell 9 for a penny instead of the original 6 for a penny. A stallholder continually found guilty of charging too much was in danger of losing his licence to sell goods altogether.

During the Middle Ages a market was perhaps the most obvious sign of a town's growing importance. It served the needs of the inhabitants and provided a base upon which further prosperity could be built.

13 (*Left*) A typical street market. Often the narrow streets were entirely blocked by stalls and people.

14 (*Right*) A day in the stocks.

Weekly markets allowed people to buy and sell goods from the surrounding areas. But for goods that could not be obtained locally, many towns held fairs. Like markets, these could only be organized with royal permission, but they were much less frequent. Usually fairs were held just once a year, most often around Michaelmas time (September) when the harvest was over and people had goods to sell and money to spend. The fairs lasted several days, sometimes weeks, and to them came merchants from all over the world.

They were certainly spectacular events. For more than a month beforehand preparations would be in progress. Goods arrived by boat or packhorse, stalls were erected and the streets decorated with brightly coloured flags. People flooded into the town, filling the taverns and boarding houses. There were farmers, their families and workers, country gentry and even foreign merchants from as far away as Italy and North Africa.

The stalls displayed all sorts of wonderful wares. Some of the goods had never been seen before in the shops of the town, and probably would not be seen again for many a year. There were French wines, Oriental spices and tapestries, Italian glassware, Damascus steel and many varieties of silk, jewellery and trinkets. How the simple country folk, up for a day in town, would gaze in amazement! There, on display, were the products of countries they had only heard talked about, or perhaps even of countries they had never heard of at all.

Every fair was strictly controlled by the authorities. All shops had to close while it was taking place and every stallholder, whether a townsman or a 'foreigner', had to abide by the laws laid down by the guilds. Many fairs grew to be famous, like those at St Ives (Huntingdonshire), Bristol, Exeter, Chester, Barnet and Edinburgh. Two of the biggest were St Giles's Fair at Winchester and Stourbridge Fair near Cambridge. Both lasted three weeks a year, and their fame spread as far as the Aegean Sea and Egypt. Some towns even gained a reputation for special articles: Birmingham Fair for onions and gingerbread, Barnet Fair for horses and Nottingham Fair, popularly called Goose Fair, for poultry.

Besides the ordinary business of buying and selling, fairs offered all the fun and excitement of a holiday. There were jugglers, fire-eaters, dancing bears, musicians, quack-doctors and fortune-tellers. Scandal was exchanged, news from distant parts was discussed, friars preached sermons and cripples exhibited their sores and begged for money. Further away, in the nearby fields, games and sports were provided, with races, quarterstaff and archery contests and wrestling matches all taking place. Gambling was rife and poor peasants, innocent of the ways of the town, might lose their entire savings on a casual bet, a turn of a card or the toss of a coin. With so many thousands gathered in one place, other aspects of town life, unfortunately, were unavoidable: disputes between traders and customers often led to fighting in the streets, and large numbers of pickpockets and cut-pursers mingled with the crowds. In fact, so

26 unseemly were the incidents at St Bartholomew's Fair at Smithfield in London that it soon became well known for its riots, rowdy behaviour and dishonesty. By Tudor times towns were firmly established. Every important settlement had its charter, its guilds, its market and its fair. It also enjoyed a fair degree of self-government, and prospered on both local and foreign trade. Neither was education neglected. By the sixteenth century there were over 200 grammar schools in England and the universities at Oxford and Cambridge had expanded almost to the size they are today. In the towns the old customs and sports of 'Merrie England' continued with increased gusto. The whipping-post for beggars and the stocks for drunkards were common sights; bear-baiting and cock-fighting provided amusement and, in the appropriate seasons, the maypole was set up and Morris dancing took place in the market square. Even football was becoming popular, although as yet it bore little relation to our modern game. A blown-up pig's bladder was used as a ball and youths would hurtle it along the narrow streets. As one writer complained in 1531, it was 'nothing but beastly fury and extreme violence, whereof proceedeth hurt, and consequently rancour and malice do remain with them that he wounded'.

The advances made in towns and town life throughout the Middle Ages blossomed under Queen Elizabeth I. London in particular took pride of place. Her great commercial connections and thriving industries made her by far England's premier town.

15 Dancing round the maypole.

Chapter 3
Urban Transition

Elizabethan London

Let us take a look at what the capital was like in the reign of Queen Elizabeth I (1558-1603).

To begin with, London then was not nearly as large as it is today. There were none of the suburbs that there are now, and even from the centre of town open fields and farmland could be seen in the distance. A fast walker could walk across the city from east to west in less than an hour; from north to south in about half that time.

In fact, Elizabethan London was not much bigger in area than its Roman predecessor. The medieval walls, in places nearly 11 metres high, had largely been built on the original Roman remains, and these still formed the rough boundary between town and country. In the south-east corner of the city stood the Norman Tower of London; what is now called London Wall was the northern border, and the Temple formed the farthest extent of development to the west. The old town gates at Ludgate, Newgate, Aldersgate, Moorgate Cripplegate, Aldgate and Bishopsgate remained in good repair and were still the principal entrances to the city. Outside the walls London had only just begun to spread out. A number of cottages and inns had grown up around each gate, and, further away, villages were beginning to expand along the main approaches to the capital.

Although Westminster was the seat of Parliament, it was still at that time a separate settlement. The only buildings between Westminster and the City of London were in the Strand which ran along the north bank of the Thames. The countryside was never very far away: places like Holborn and Whitechapel were still open and largely unspoilt, whilst at Smithfield, on the edge of town, a weekly cattle market was held.

The River Thames was much wider than it is today and formed the southern boundary of the city. The opposite bank was marshy and had a mere scattering of buildings. London Bridge was the only bridge along the entire stretch of this part of the river. Supported by a total of 18 arches and crowned with a double row of shops and houses, this was one of the wonders of London. It formed, in fact, a street as busy as any in the city itself.

16 A view of Elizabethan London. Notice the traitors' heads spiked over the gate to London Bridge.

Despite its relatively small size, there is no doubt that Elizabethan London was a major commercial centre. Nowhere else in England was there a town with such power, independence and wealth. Merchants from all over Europe flocked there, either to trade on behalf of their masters or to settle permanently and make fortunes for themselves. Between 1500 and 1600, London's population more than doubled, from 75,000 people to 200,000 people. By the end of Elizabeth's reign in 1603, it had become not only by far the most important city in Britain but also the country's centre for all European commerce. In every way it was truly a great city.

Sailing in from the coast along the broad sweep of the Thames, the visitor would be struck immediately by the wealth, beauty and activity of London. Clustering around the tall tower of the old St Paul's Cathedral, whose spire was destroyed by lightning in 1561, the city was indeed a wonderful sight. Over 100 church spires dominated the skyline; towers and turrets stood out like castles above the red roofs, and colourful flags and bunting fluttered in the air. The river was crowded with all types of craft: flat boats and barges loaded down with goods and passengers; small rowing boats ferrying backwards and forwards from bank to bank; and tall-masted merchantmen hoisting their white sails and bound for foreign parts. All along the waterfront stood large and busy wharves, their cranes active unloading strange and marvellous goods: citrus fruits from the Mediterranean, spices from Asia and tobacco from the newly discovered lands of America. Then, further upstream along the Strand, were the elegant homes of the gentry with their great leaded windows, red brick walls and tall, decorated chimneys. Each had its long well-kept garden sloping down to the river, the lawns and flower-beds leading to high wrought-iron gates where a flight of steps ran down into the water. In the distance, the mighty Palace of Westminster and the Abbey loomed up, their turrets rising high above the jumble of black-and-white cottages around them.

Everywhere there was the appearance of wealth. The shops were busy, their open counters displaying all varieties of fine goods to attract the passers-by. The different traders — grocers, booksellers, apothecaries and so on — still flourished as they clustered together in their own streets. Names like Pudding Lane, Goldsmith's Row and Meat Street still survive to tell us of their former significance. In other ways, too, there were signs that prosperity had come. The newly built Royal Exchange now became the centre for commerce, while down Fleet Street the Temple was fast becoming famous as a college for lawyers. Neither was there apparently a shortage of money. Merchants, lords and their ladies, guild officials, craftsmen and even ordinary shopkeepers walked about in their fine ruffles and laces, brightly coloured silks, satins and velvets. Even the houses were richly built — thick oak beams with fillings of brick or lath and plaster, and small latticed windows of leaded glass. The overhanging upper storeys made the streets dark, but they were brightly painted and so heavily carved that no-one could doubt the social standing of those who lived within.

But not all London showed the same prosperous face. Next to the fine churches and palaces, the parks and riverside walks and the quaint old courtyards and houses, there was a much more unpleasant aspect of town life. Many of the streets were wide and well paved with cobblestones or flagstones, but others were narrow, dark and muddy. The inhabitants still emptied their slops out of the windows and sewage still collected in the gutters. The smells were dreadful, flies infested every corner, and hordes of rats ran about at will among the buildings. On hot days so overwhelming was the stench and so disease-ridden the streets that the womenfolk remained indoors.

And the noise was as bad as the smell. All day long the streets were jammed with traffic. Goods' carts, carriages, two-wheeled curricles and ladies' sedan chairs hurried in all directions. Horses and mules clattered across the cobbles and great iron-rimmed wheels scraped the stones. Above the noise of the traffic, from all sides, came the hoarse cries of hawkers and costermongers. Pedlars or chapmen stood with laden trays hung round their necks displaying all manner of wares, shouting 'Lily white vinegar', 'Have you any old boots?', 'New brooms, green brooms', or 'White-hearted cabbages'. Apprentices stood at their masters' shop doorways touting for custom and greeting each passer-by with a coarse-voiced, 'What lack you sir?'. Balled singers could be heard declaiming from the song sheets they were selling, and, further away, town criers were shouting out the local news to those interested enough to listen.

Even water was sold on the streets. London was provided with some piped water, pumps and wells, but there was still a shortage. Hawkers used to walk about the streets with a large wooden bucket or barrel slung over their shoulder, filling with water the container of anyone who paid the farthing or halfpenny charge. The cry of 'Clubs', however, did not mean that clubs were being sold. This signalled the start of a street brawl and, at the first sound of it, crowds of apprentices would rush from their shops to watch or take part in the fight. The Elizabethan playwright Thomas Dekker (1570-1641) has left us this description of London in his day:

> In every street, carts and coaches make such a thundering as if the world ran upon wheels. At every corner, men, women and children meet in such shoals that posts are set up . . . to strengthen the houses, lest with jostling one another they should shoulder them down. Besides, hammers are beating in one place, tubs hooping in another, pots clinking in a third, water tankards running at a tilt in a fourth. Here are porters sweating under burdens, there, merchant's men bearing bags of money. Chapmen (as if they were at leapfrog) skip out of one shop into another. Tradesmen . . . are lusty at legs and never stand still.

17 A Tudor clothes' shop.   **18** A water-carrier.

Londoners in those days were not particularly either sensitive or religious. The fact that St Paul's Cathedral was one of the finest churches in Europe did not prevent them from abusing it dreadfully. By this time it had become nothing more nor less than a centre for social and commercial gatherings, or, as one writer put it, 'a house of talking, of walking, of brawling, of minstrelsy, of hawks and of dogs'. The central aisle was more like a market place, with merchants, costers and beggars all milling around in general confusion. In some corners shopkeepers set up makeshift stalls and used the tombs as counters over which to conclude their money transactions. To add to the noise, horses and mules were led through the cathedral transepts since these provided a short-cut to the stables. Even the churchyard outside was not left untouched; here among the gravestones was situated London's main book market.

But if London during the day was bad, London at night was worse. Oil lamps were lit and hung up outside the larger houses to give a rough form of street lighting, but this was very dim and did little to improve the long, dark alleyways. Vagabonds, thieves and murderers roamed the streets waylaying innocent passers-by, and gangs of thugs moved from tavern to tavern stealing from the helpless drunks as they staggered from the bright, crowded rooms into the dark night. Late revellers, on their way home, were in danger of having their throats cut or their eyes pierced out; the lucky might only be beaten up and left to crawl to the nearest house for help. The late walker could avoid the

19 Night watchmen.

darkest corners by keeping to the middle of the road, but this only increased his chances of stumbling accidentally into the sewage channel.

To combat crime, watchmen toured the streets all night carrying lanterns and calling out each hour as it passed. 'Three o'clock and all's well!' might have woken those in bed, but to those still about it held a welcome promise of safety, at least for the time being. Constables were also appointed to patrol the streets but their lot was not a happy one. They were just as likely to be attacked and robbed as anyone else — more so, in fact, since they were not particularly popular among the criminal classes.

Punishments in those days were as brutal as the crimes. A common sight in Elizabethan London was a man being dragged through the streets to the gallows at Tyburn (close to where Marble Arch now stands). There he would be hanged for a few minutes, taken down while still living, drawn or stretched, and then quartered, his limbs being cut off one by one. On top of Temple Bar, and on the gateway to London Bridge, there were always the spiked heads of traitors, some recently cut with blood running down the cheeks, others more decomposed with the white bones sticking out through the decaying flesh. The prisons — and there were many around London — were forever full. Those at Cripplegate, Ludgate and Newgate were particularly notorious. Cells were cold, damp and dark, and many prisoners were chained up for months at a time and often left to die.

20 The Globe Theatre, Southwark.

Executions at the Tower and hangings at Tyburn provided Londoners with regular entertainment, but other entertainments, fortunately, were more wholesome. Puppet shows were given regularly along Fleet Street, there was a zoo at the Tower of London, and, over the river at Southwark, the Bear Garden gave people room to drink, talk and play games. Miracle plays were still performed by the guilds on holy days, but more popular now were the newer type of plays being put on at the taverns and recently-built theatres. William Shakespeare had already made a name for himself over at the Globe Theatre in Southwark, and was fast becoming the most famous playwright in the country. Everywhere new playhouses were springing up as people sought alternatives to the old amusements of bear-baiting, cock-fighting and trials of strength.

In Elizabethan London, all forms of town life existed side by side. Aristocrats and their lady wives, rich merchants, craftsmen and beggars all jostled each other in the streets. The sweet smell of perfumes and flowers mingled with the overpowering stench of the sewers. The palaces of the rich were built within a stone's throw of the hovels of the poor. The noise level and crime rate were both extremely high, but this did not stop people from coming from far and wide to live in London, and with any luck to make there their fortune. The streets may have been muddy and full of rats, but to the hopeful newcomers they were paved with gold.

The seventeenth century was essentially a period of change. At the end of the Elizabethan era English towns were still largely medieval — in appearance, in commercial terms and socially. Most towns were very small: London was more than five times larger than its nearest rivals. By the end of the Stuart period, however, a century later, all this had changed. London was still dominant but now other towns had begun to catch up. Their trade and industries were flourishing, their populations were growing rapidly and town life was developing into something far more advanced. In particular, the seventeenth century saw the beginnings of classical architecture, town planning, the growth of suburbs and a more cultured town society.

Despite the political troubles between Crown and Parliament, economically Britain prospered during the seventeenth century. The woollen cloth industry continued to be the most important source of income, as it had been right through the Middle Ages, but other industries were beginning to develop. In Yorkshire and South Wales towns grew up around the small open-cast pits where coal was being dug for the first time, and in Northumberland Newcastle was expanding with the profits from sea-coal. Much of this coal was used in the new iron and steel industries, for which supplies of pig-iron were imported from Sweden. Birmingham and Sheffield, especially, benefited from this new technology. Sheffield specialized in cutlery and such was its success that during the century its population more than doubled. The cotton industry, too, was expanding. Using supplies of raw cotton from Asia, the mills of Lancashire switched from making woollens to cotton cloth production. Liverpool, above all, reaped the benefit of this and became extremely prosperous.

Trade also flourished. The trading companies founded in Tudor times, like the Merchant Adventurers and the Levant Company, now increased in importance and extended their spheres of influence. In addition to these, new companies were formed like the Hudson's Bay Company (to trade with Canada) and the Royal African Company. Perhaps the greatest of all was the East India Company, founded in 1600 to encourage trade with Asia. This became the richest and most influential company of all, and in the following century was largely responsible for the spread of the British Empire into India.

Other factors, too, led to Britain's economic prosperity. Successful industries meant that more capital was invested and this in turn encouraged industrial expansion. The banking system developed, and the buying and selling of securities became an important financial practice. In 1694 the Bank of England was set up, and two years later a recoinage helped to make the value of our currency more stable.

Mass immigration into England towards the end of the seventeenth century gave added impetus to town growth. Many thousands of French protestants, called Huguenots, fled from the persecutions of King Louis XIV and settled in this country. Here they established or improved many industries including paper, linen, glass, clocks and the famous silk manufacturing industry at

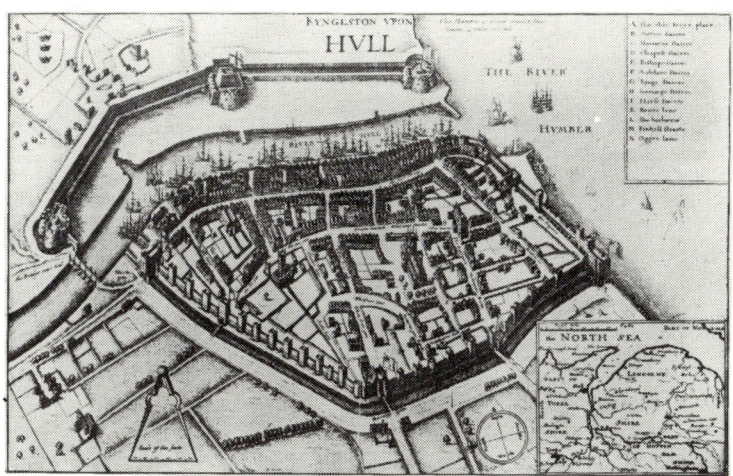

21 This engraving of 1665 shows Hull as a busy port. The river is thronged with ships.

Coventry and Macclesfield. By the end of the seventeenth century England possessed several major industrial and commercial towns. Bristol and Norwich had over 30,000 inhabitants each; Hull grew with its whaling and fishing industries; Liverpool and Plymouth developed strong trading links with the American colonies, and Whitby, Yarmouth and Harwich acquired large shipbuilding yards.

Perhaps the most important change of all during the Stuart age was the introduction of classicism into English architecture. Foreign travel had become fashionable, and the Grand Tour — up to two years spent travelling abroad — was considered essential to round off every rich gentleman's education. Young men everywhere were more knowledgeable; they learned foreign languages, studied European politics, and fostered a liking for all aspects of European culture. Young architects and designers, especially, became interested in the ancient Roman ruins in Italy and southern France, and in the work of such men as Michelangelo and Leonardo da Vinci who had been designing in the classical style a century or so previously. They came home to put their new ideas into practice.

One such architect was Inigo Jones, who is generally thought to have been the first Englishman to bring the Renaissance or classical style to this country. His two most famous surviving buildings are the Banqueting House in London's Whitehall, which was finished in 1622, and the Queen's House at Greenwich, completed in 1635. These new buildings were very distinctive and, at that time, quite novel. They had no towers or turrets but were shaped like square blocks with flat façades, large rectangular windows and flat roofs hidden from sight. The decoration was similar to that found on old Roman buildings and included balustrades, columns and pediments (triangular-shaped blocks of stone over doors and windows). They were symmetrically planned with perfect proportions.

36 The Rebuilding of London

The urban changes of the seventeenth century were at their most apparent in London.

Ever since the Black Death, plague had made repeated appearances in England, particularly in towns, where the lack of sanitation and the cramped living conditions encouraged its spread. London, as we have seen, was far from clean, and in 1665 it was visited by possibly the worst outbreak of plague for nearly 200 years. Many thousands perished, and in just a few months one-fifth of the capital's entire population was killed. In the following year came the Great Fire, which many people believed was God-sent to rid the city of its deadly germs. For five days early in September 1666, fire raged across London, the flames devouring everything within their path. The result: St Paul's Cathedral together with 84 other churches destroyed, and over 400 streets razed to the ground. Never, since the burning of ancient Rome, had such a disaster struck so great a city. The rebuilding of London that followed gave new impetus both to the city's growth and to the classical movement in architecture.

Sir Christopher Wren put forward plans for an entirely new capital. The design he proposed was not dissimilar to that of old Roman towns: a pattern of rectangles with straight, wide streets, squares and tree-lined avenues, all in the classical style. Unfortunately, lack of money forced King Charles II and his advisers to turn down these very radical plans, and rebuilding took place instead largely on the old layout. Many of the narrow, dark streets and irregular building plots were retained.

Some parts of London, however, did receive a new look. Where the old wooden-framed houses had been destroyed, large, spacious, brick ones were built in their place. In the former open spaces, too, new houses appeared, new squares and new terraces all with the typical classical features. The rebuilt London was much more elegant than the old and, as Sir John Reresby tells us, did not take very long to construct:

> The dreadful effects of the fire were not so strange as the rebuilding of this great city, which by reason of the King's and Parliament's care, and the great wealth and opulency of the city itself, was rebuilded most stately with brick (the greatest part being before nothing but lath and lime) in four or five years' time.

Above all this there arose a new skyline. Although Christopher Wren's plan for an entirely new city had been rejected, he was still given the task of rebuilding many of London's churches. And what wonderful churches they were! Over 50 were built, including St Clement Danes and St Mary-le-Bow, all with fine classical features and tall, distinctive spires soaring up into the sky. In the centre stood Wren's masterpiece — St Paul's Cathedral, its great dome rising to 112 metres and its white Portland stonework gleaming in the sunshine.

The Fire also caused London to spread outwards. During rebuilding shopkeepers and merchants moved away to continue business outside the walls. Once areas were settled in this way they seldom reverted back to countryside again. Streets, houses, shops and warehouses sprang up, and London acquired her first real suburbs. By the end of the century the capital's population reached half a million. Westminster was joined to the city, and in every direction London spread out. In the west it stretched as far as Hyde Park, to the north Tottenham Court Road, and to the east it reached Stepney. South of the Thames Lambeth and Rotherhithe had joined Southwark as part of the metropolis.

Under the Stuart kings town life changed as well. The guilds still survived, but the local government of each town became detached from commerce and more independent of the merchants. Many towns, like London, had already developed a system of local elections whereby the inhabitants were able to vote for their own town councils. Newspapers began to appear. At first these were just single-sheet newsletters giving information about coach timetables, lost property and the latest political news. Soon, however, publications like the *Tatler*, the *Spectator* and the *Examiner* were printing not only news but also articles of a much wider interest: on the theatre, horse-racing, Court topics and business investments.

More than anything else, Stuart times saw the break-up of medieval town life and heralded the coming of a new age.

22 London's new skyline, dominated by the dome of Wren's St Paul's.

Chapter 4
Georgian Towns

An Age of Improvement

In history, progress and change do not always continue at the same pace. Sometimes many centuries may pass without any important advance in the way people live, at other times a few years may witness a complete revolution. As we have seen earlier in the book, the period of the Saxons, called the Dark Ages, was a time when progress was relatively slow. So too, though to a lesser extent, were the Middle Ages. But the eighteenth century, during the greater part of which the Hanoverian Georges were on the throne, was quite different. Progress was rapid. The social and economic changes which occurred under the Stuarts had laid the foundations for perhaps the most significant period in our history. In almost every way the Georgian age was an age of improvement.

In less than 100 years Britain was fundamentally altered. Nowhere was this more obvious than in the towns. Classical architecture blossomed, roads were improved, transport became easier and faster, and the rich were enabled to lead more comfortable lives. Before the end of the century new industries were developing, new factories were being built, and trade with the British Empire and with Europe was bringing to England wealth previously unimagined. The population doubled between 1700 and 1800, rising from about 6 million to 12 million. Towns were flourishing with a new impetus and expanding with almost unlimited speed.

At the beginning of the century, England was still a predominantly rural country. In particular, transport was no better than it had been for centuries; people could still travel no faster than a horse could gallop. The roads were generally just dirt tracks: hard, cracked and rutted in summer; muddy and sometimes impassable in winter. When not walking or on horseback people travelled in carriages but these were uncomfortable and often so badly designed that they regularly broke down. Travelling in them was a nightmare. The bumpy ride from London to Bath might take four days, London to York six or seven days.

This poor transport meant that there was little contact between different towns. Most people lived and died in the settlement of their birth, never having ventured further afield than the nearest market or fair — perhaps a distance of

23 A Georgian street scene. Sedan chairs could be hired like taxi-cabs can today.

ten or twenty miles. To the farmer, peasant or country squire, the large towns and cities were like foreign lands. News travelled very slowly, and newspapers could take a week or more to reach the isolated rural population, if they did at all. In any event, few people could either read or write.

By the end of the eighteenth century, however, much of this had changed. The coming of the turnpike system, above all, brought England's towns closer together. Hundreds of miles of new roads, all well drained and well surfaced, were built to link the main commercial and fashionable centres. These, together with better designed and more comfortable carriages, made travelling faster and much more pleasant. The new mail coach — the fastest vehicle of all — cut the journey between London and Bath to just a single night; between Newcastle and London to only two days. No longer were towns isolated from the rest of the country.

Improvements were also taking place inside the towns. The Georgian age saw the development of the idea of 'good taste', and this was reflected in all aspects of life: in clothes, jewellery, furniture, ornaments and manners. It was also reflected in architecture. Architects like Nicholas Hawksmoor, Sir John Vanbrugh and, later, the Adam brothers followed in the footsteps of Inigo Jones and Christopher Wren, and new classical buildings were erected all over the country. The love of uniformity and symmetry led also to a revival of town-planning which, like the buildings, echoed the style of Roman towns. Streets and roads ran in straight lines and at right-angles to each other, and building plots were rectangular. Terraces became common and largely superseded the detached houses of the past. The new terraced houses were usually four-storeyed, with a semi-basement, the main rooms on the first floor and smaller rooms like bedrooms on the two upper floors. The front door was reached up flights of steps from the pavement, and sash windows replaced the older casement type.

In London, crescents and squares were built in many parts of the city, and areas like Bloomsbury, St James's and Piccadilly acquired new dignity in the midst of an otherwise untidy and congested urban sprawl. Other improvements also took place. In the main roads paving stones replaced cobbles; and the central channels, which were formerly more like sewers, were covered over. Hanging trade-signs were removed from the shop-fronts, more streets were given names and houses were numbered. Even water closets came into use although these were only partially successful. The sewage was led hygienically through new underground pipes, though it was still emptied untreated into the river. This was unfortunate for those who lived farther downstream since the river was being used at that time to supply drinking water. Consequently typhoid and other similar diseases were rampant.

During the eighteenth century the capital's population rose from ½ million to 1½ million, and this led to serious problems of congestion. To make way for the increased traffic all the ancient gates to the city, except Temple Bar, were removed, and new bridges were thrown across the river: Westminster Bridge in 1750, Blackfriars Bridge shortly after. Even the shops on London Bridge were demolished to make room for the greater number of carriages, carts and horses. By 1800 London was the largest and busiest city in western Europe.

24 A Georgian coaching yard. The removal firm of Pickfords survives to this day.

25 The elegant Somerset Buildings in Milsom Street, Bath. Notice the sash windows, the Corinthian columns, and, along the roofline, the balustrade and pediments.

The great wealth which had been accumulating in Britain since about 1650, as a result of the increase in trade and industry, brought into being a much more numerous upper class. While the poor worked harder and for longer hours, the rich became more idle and more eager to find new ways of spending their leisure time. When in the country they went riding, fox-hunting and shooting; when in town they frequented the chocolate and coffee houses. These had first appeared in the Stuart period when increased foreign trade brought new beverages to this country. Now, in the eighteenth century, they became firmly established as urban institutions.

London by this time was not only the centre of England in commercial and political terms, but also of her literary, intellectual and fashionable life. Thus, while chocolate and coffee houses existed in most towns, those found in London were the largest and most famous. In fact, such was their popularity that by the middle of the century there were more than 500 of them in the capital alone.

The coffee houses were particularly popular. They provided a quiet, friendly atmosphere and pleasant surroundings where men could relax, gossip, read the newspapers, write letters, or just sit and smoke or take snuff. One writer explained how they were extremely convenient places, because

> You have all Manner of News there: you have a good Fire which you may sit by as long as you please: you have a Dish of Coffee, you meet your friends for the Transaction of Business, and all for a Penny, if you don't care to spend more.

Since ladies were not allowed into coffee houses the furnishings could be very simple. Only rugs covered the bare floorboards, the walls were plain, and ordinary wooden chairs were set about small, separate tables. The coffee was served in large, wide-brimmed cups; spittoons were in constant use, and the air was invariably heavy with the smell of pipe tobacco.

However, if the surroundings and facilities were commonplace, the society which patronized these coffee houses certainly was not. Men from all walks of life came there to talk freely regardless of social barriers. For hours on end they would discuss politics, religion, art, literature, music and any other subject of interest.

Soon various coffee houses became the haunts of particular groups of people. Tory politicians, for example, tended to gather at White's Chocolate House, while Whigs went to St James's Coffee House nearby. Edward Lloyd's coffee house in Lombard Street, established in the reign of Queen Anne, was frequented by people with shipping interests and developed into a major centre for all marine business. Later it became the renowned Lloyd's insurance company. Other coffee houses were well-known in the artistic and literary world as the resorts of the famous. At Wills's, near Covent Garden, the poets

John Dryden and Alexander Pope were frequent visitors, while down the road in St Martin's Lane, Old Slaughter's became the favourite meeting place of artists like Sir Joshua Reynolds, George Romney, Thomas Gainsborough and William Hogarth. And naturally, where the famous went, their friends, admirers and hangers-on followed, in the hope of being spoken to or of hearing some brilliant piece of conversation, epigram or flash of wit. Once a coffee house had been officially 'recognized' by a well-known personality, its subsequent success was assured.

However, the success of the coffee houses led ultimately to their own downfall. Increasing profits caused many owners to demolish their premises and rebuild on a much larger and grander scale. Prices were raised to pay for these alterations and in many cases a yearly subscription was charged which only the wealthy could afford. In this way many coffee houses were gradually transformed into clubs.

By the 1770s, clubs had largely superseded coffee houses as the resorts of fashionable society. But they were far more exclusive than their predecessors and generally far more luxurious. For an annual subscription of five or ten guineas, members were provided with all the best: carpets and expensive wallpapers, soft armchairs and settees, and scores of servants.

Like the coffee houses, each club tended to be frequented by a particular interest group. Catholics who remained loyal to the exiled Stuart royal family set up the Cocoa Tree Club, while, in opposition, Protestants who swore allegiance to the Hanoverians founded the Kit-Kat Club. The Beef-Steak in Fleet Street became the main literary club, where people like Dr Johnson, David Garrick the actor and Henry Fielding the writer would go to eat, drink and argue about their respective professions.

Clubs also became hives of card playing. In the Georgian age gambling was an obsession, and rich young men would wager on almost anything, however absurd. There were many gambling pursuits, such as cock-fighting, boxing contests and horse-racing, but cards were the most popular. Wherever a group of men came together a game of cards would be started, and it did not take long for clubs like Almack's, White's and Brooks's to acquire notoriety as gambling establishments. To their members, playing cards was an extremely serious business and required a great deal of preparation. According to one writer:

They began by pulling off their embroidered coats, put on frieze great-coats, or turned their coats inside outwards for luck. They put on pieces of leather, such as worn by footmen when they clean knives, to save their lace ruffles; and to guard their eyes from the light, and to prevent tumbling their hair, wore high-crowned straw hats with broad brims adorned with flowers and ribbons, and masks to conceal their emotions when they played at Quinze.

Once suitably dressed, they would gamble well into the night and often right through till breakfast the following day. And the stakes were often large. A letter written in 1770 and referring to Almack's describes how:

> the young men of the age lose ten, fifteen, twenty thousand pounds in an evening there. Lord Stavordale, not one-and-twenty, lost £11,000 there last Tuesday, but recovered it by one great hand at Hazard.

But many were not as lucky as Lord Stavordale. Sometimes entire fortunes would be lost in a single night. A man might lose his money, his estate, his carriages and even his servants and be left destitute by morning. Yet to take such disasters with good grace was considered essential etiquette. After losing most of his fortune, the politician Charles James Fox sat down calmly in a chair to read a book; and he was no exception. The world might fall apart and the heavens collapse, but the eighteenth-century gentleman would remain his usual imperturbable self.

26 A rich young man's good reputation might depend entirely upon how many bottles of wine he could consume. Here a link-boy is offering to light a young buck home through the dark streets. 1823.

You must put yourself into good sharp training in order to become a four bottle man, as soon as you are able to support the Title with credit; you will find it to your advantage, to attend public dinners, where the value r... ...ved will quadruple the price of your ticket; and you may turn out, a walking wine cellar.

Most people in this country today do not usually consume exorbitant quantities of alcohol. Beer and other drinks are enjoyed in public houses, and wine is drunk with some meals but, by and large, the British are a relatively sober race. However, this has not always been true, and was certainly not the case in Georgian England.

In those days neither tea nor coffee was the national beverage. Although the coffee houses and clubs were popular and much frequented, they did not replace the taverns and inns which were so much a part of 'Old England'. They merely provided an alternative source of entertainment for those with time and money to spare. For most working people the public house or tavern remained the most important institution in a dull and uneventful life.

During the eighteenth century the range of alcoholic drinks available increased enormously. Before, there had been the usual home-brewed beers and ciders together with — for the rich at least — a small selection of European wines. Now, apart from ales, all kinds of liqueurs came on the market, a wide range of French and Italian wines, both table and dessert, and various spirits like brandy and whisky. Moreover, the general rise in wealth among the upper and middle classes combined with the relative cheapness of strong drinks resulted in a staggering increase in the consumption of alcohol.

The rich could afford the more expensive drinks, and their long leisure hours enabled them to drink a great deal over extended periods. Punch, madeira, brandy and port were consumed in stupendous amounts. 'Lemonade', too, became very popular amongst the hardened drinkers; not surprisingly since this, unlike what we now call lemonade, was made of equal parts of brandy, white wine and water, with half a lemon added.

But if the wealthy could afford such drinks the poor certainly could not. They, instead, drank beer and gin. Ever since the Middle Ages public houses had acted as social centres for the working classes. It was here that men could come for company, a chat, some peace away from nagging wives and screaming children, or just to drown their sorrows. It was often here too that men received their wages and could pawn their few belongings for odd coppers. Now, in Georgian times, alehouses became the mainstay of working-class life to an even greater extent. They began to serve as employment exchanges where the unemployed gathered and where employers came to recruit men for vacant positions. Since the changes taking place in agriculture and industry had led to high unemployment, alehouses served in this way a very important function.

Beer was cheap and plentiful. Men would drink it all day long, and it was quite usual for a person to consume as many as five, six or seven pints in a single session without any serious after-effects. In the 1720s the American statesman Benjamin Franklin, while working in a London printing office, wrote:

> My companion at press drank every day a pint of beer before breakfast, a pint at breakfast, a pint between breakfast and dinner, a pint in the afternoon about six o'clock and another pint when he had done his day's work.

As the century wore on a new and more obnoxious drink gained popularity among the working classes: gin. This was distilled in ever increasing quantities and sold for next to nothing, and soon it had ousted beer as the main thirst-quencher of the poor. Known variously as 'Madame Geneva', 'Blue Ruin' or 'Strip-me-naked', it was an evil-smelling, evil-tasting liquid. Made as it was from the cheapest possible ingredients and containing large quantities of raw alcohol, its effects were devastating. From exhilaration and happiness the drinker rapidly declined into a state of dizziness, with head pains, vomiting and eventual unconsciousness. In comparison, the effects of beer were positively harmless!

Gin represented an escape from a life of hunger and drudgery and it is easy to understand how a poor person could succumb to it. Men, women and children alike fell under its evil influence. Neither did the government help. There was only a small tax on gin and no licence was needed to sell it to the public. So cheap was it, and so popular, that by the 1740s it was estimated that one house in every four in London was a gin-shop. Over doorways everywhere signs proclaimed the sale of cheap gin: 'Drunk for a penny, dead drunk for two pence, clean straw for nothing' was a typical one.

With gin drinking the urban poor reached new depths of degradation. Crimes of murder and theft multiplied by leaps and bounds, committed either by those seeking money enough to buy the liquor, or by those already drunk on it. There is a story told of a girl who took her little child away from the workhouse so that she could strangle him and then sell his clothes for money to buy gin. Such instances were not rare. London was full of beggars, cripples and criminals under the influence of gin and making the streets foul and dangerous. Unsightly bodies, their eyes bloodshot and bulging and their faces bloated, lay about the gutters in a drunken stupor, the smell of their breath polluting the air. Gin drinking was more than just an outlet for depressed lives: it was a disease which led only to death.

In 1751 the government finally decided to put a high tax on spirits, and gin became generally too expensive for the poor to buy. But much of the damage, in terms both of social and moral decline, had already been done.

BEER STREET.

Beer, happy Produce of our Isle
Can sinewy Strength impart,
And wearied with Fatigue and Toil
Can cheer each manly Heart.

Designed by W. Hogarth.

Labour and Art upheld by Thee
Successfully advance,
We quaff Thy balmy Juice with Glee
And Water leave to France.

Published according to Act of Parliament Feb.y 1. 1751.

Genius of Health, thy grateful Taste
Rivals the Cup of Jove,
And warms each English generous Breast
With Liberty and Love.

Price 1s.

27 Beer Street by William Hogarth. Here the lower classes are enjoying their mugs of ale. Gin drinking had far worse effects.

The dreadful conditions under which the poor lived were of little interest to the upper classes, who were for the most part idle, pleasure-loving people, caring little for the troubles of others. As far as they were concerned, the towns could be riddled with poverty, hunger, disease and drunkenness, yet provided such hardships passed them by they were happy. For many of the rich, life was one continuous round of coffee houses and clubs, parties and dinners, drinking, gambling and travel.

But this existence, pleasant as it may sound, was not without its drawbacks. Excesses of food and drink took their toll, and indigestion, headaches, skin infections and gout became common complaints. Increasingly the upper classes began to look for possible cures, and when the pain was bad any suggestion, however unusual, was willingly tried. In particular, spa towns and, later, seaside resorts were developed as centres for health and good living.

The health-giving properties of certain springs had been known since earliest times, and the Romans, while in England, had done much to develop and use them. After the departure of the Romans, however, many of these springs had fallen into disuse or even been forgotten altogether. It was not until now, in the eighteenth century, that they once again became social attractions.

People teemed to the springs in their thousands, hoping every one of them that their ailments would be cured. According to contemporary advertisements, the waters were:

> a Sovereign Remedy against all Faintings, Sweatings, Lowness of Spirits etc . . . or Disorders proceeding from Intemperance, eating of Fruit, drinking of bad wine or any other poysonous or crude liquors.

To the springs too came hordes of doctors, quacks and charlatans to provide medical advice — at a price — and to sell their dubious mixtures to an unsuspecting public.

Wherever there were health-giving springs a town would expand to cater for the visitors. In the summer months, especially, crowds flocked to the spas. Hotels were erected and quickly filled; new shops were opened; new theatres and Assembly Rooms were planned and new houses built. Epsom, Tunbridge Wells and Cheltenham grew with unparalleled speed while, in the north, Buxton and Harrogate suddenly blossomed into fashionable centres. Even the middle classes — shopkeepers, business people and the like — started to want to visit springs, and, for them, smaller spa towns developed. Around London, for example, Hampstead, Richmond and Islington catered for those not wealthy enough to go further afield.

The spa towns provided a wide variety of amusements, and very soon people were visiting them not just for a cure but for a holiday as well. A typical day might begin with a visit to the baths where the ailing would soak themselves, sometimes up to their necks. After changing into dry clothes they would drink the waters in the Pump Room, and then breakfast, with a light meal of cold meats, fish and coffee, in the Assembly Room. This would be followed, perhaps, by a visit to the local church for the morning service. For the rest of the day the visitors could please themselves. They could stroll in the gardens, visit friends, go shopping or read quietly in the library. The evenings were more festive: there were balls, theatres and gaming tables to choose from. With the eating and drinking that went on it was quite common for people to undo in the evening all the work they had put in so conscientiously in the morning. Not that this worried them unduly; after all, they were there to enjoy themselves and this they intended to do to the best of their ability.

By far the most popular, fashionable and largest spa town was Bath, with its naturally hot springs. Built on the old Roman town of Aquae Sulis, Bath quickly became the focal point of aristocratic circles. Under its Master of Ceremonies Richard Nash, known as 'Beau Nash', the city was transformed from a provincial backwater to the most thriving town in western England. Nash organized all the entertainments, supervised the running of the Pump Room and Gaming Rooms, and introduced a complete new code of conduct, manners and etiquette. It was he, too, who encouraged the paving of the roads and made the first ever real attempt at proper street lighting with lanterns set up at regular intervals throughout the town. Such was his authority that he became known as the 'King of Bath', and few people dared to ignore his strict regulations. On one occasion George II's daughter, Amelia, asked for an extension of a ball beyond eleven o'clock. The fact that she was a royal princess made not the slightest difference to his reply: 'I reign here and my laws *must* be kept'.

28 'The Comforts of Bath', by Thomas Rowlandson. The ailing take the waters in the Pump Room.

50   From taking spring water for health reasons to taking sea-water for the same purpose was only a short step. Since the beginning of the century doctors like the eminent Dr Russell and Dr Shaw had been prescribing sea bathing and sea-water drinking as the cure for all sorts of ills from melancholia and disorders of the stomach to vertigo and scrofula. Soon the coast was dotted with new seaside resorts. Scarborough was one of the first, to be followed later by a whole range of others: Margate, Weymouth, Southend, Lyme Regis, Deal, Eastbourne and Portsmouth. Here not only the rich but the middle classes came to be healed, to rest and to enjoy themselves. At first people just drank the sea-water, too timid to bathe and only occasionally daring enough to paddle up to their ankles. Gradually, however, bathing became more the 'done' thing and both men and women were soon taking dips in the nude. A new invention was used as a changing room: the bathing machine. At Margate Richard Pococke described:

> the conveniency of covered carriages at the end of which there is a covering that lets down with hoops, so that people can go down a ladder into the water and not be seen, and those who please may jump in and swim.

29 Bathing machines at Bridlington Bay, Yorkshire, 1813.

Just as Bath became the most successful of the spa towns, so Brighton was the most popular seaside resort. Within a few years the tiny fishing village known as Brighthelmstone had blossomed into a thriving holiday town. The fishermen's old pebble cottages were pulled down to make room for the elegant new houses of the rich. These incorporated all the finest features of contemporary architecture: bow windows and balconies, charming drawing rooms and small front gardens railed in by decorative wrought-iron work. Towards the end of the century the Prince of Wales, later King George IV, was a regular visitor to Brighton, and this further encouraged the town's development. The Pavilion — the Prince's summer residence — became a centre of attraction, and the heart of the town's cultured and fashionable world. As far away as Paris, Brighton was the bye-word for English civilization and society. One poet wrote:

Tis at Brighton, the mirror of watering places,
Assemble their Honours, their Lordships and Graces,
Nay, England's first Prince — and the famous Dame Fitz*
And old friends meet new friends of fashion and wit.
*[Mrs Maria Fitzherbert whom the Prince of Wales secretly married in 1785]

In the peaceful, elegant and fashionable surroundings of these spa towns and seaside resorts, the world must have seemed a contented place. Here, there was little evidence that England was now entering one of the most important and fundamental upheavals of her entire history.

30 The Steyne at Brighton in 1824. The pier, boat trips and donkey rides were already becoming seaside attractions. Notice the fine Regency buildings.

Characters on the Steyne Brighton.

Chapter 5
Industrial Towns

New Inventions

Through the eighteenth century progress was more rapid in Britain than anywhere else in the world. In both agriculture and industry hundreds of new inventions were introduced. These had far-reaching effects, not least of which was the appearance of the first real industrial towns.

Improvements in farming — which were all part of the Agricultural Revolution — were long overdue. Methods of cultivation had changed little since Roman times. Now, at last, new farm machinery and rearing techniques were making possible a much more efficient system. Yields of grain and root crops more than doubled, and livestock became bigger, healthier and more meaty.

At the same time there were great improvements in industry, especially in textile manufacturing and in iron- and steel-making where the use of machinery increased production by up to four or five times.

There is not space enough here to give many details of the Industrial Revolution. But certain inventions do stand out as being of particular significance to the development of towns. One of these was Samuel Crompton's 'mule', first introduced in 1779. This was a type of loom capable of spinning fine thread on a large scale and at a fairly low cost. This meant that it was no longer economical for textiles to be made by hand by women at home. Cloth manufacturing ceased to be widely dispersed, and instead developed in a few larger centres where workers and machinery could be supervised in greater numbers.

In the iron and steel industry the major breakthrough was Abraham Darby's introduction of coke for smelting. Before, charcoal had been used, and this had naturally meant that all the furnaces — and therefore the centres of the industry — were sited in the main forested areas such as the Weald in Sussex, the New Forest in Hampshire and the Forest of Dean in Gloucestershire. Now, however, the coalfields developed as centres for iron and steel, and production increased rapidly.

As more power was needed so the demand for coke and coal expanded. This meant that new coal-pits had to be opened up. Where the old surface pits could

31 Dark, crowded, smoky towns grew rapidly during the Industrial Revolution. This engraving of Wolverhampton gives some idea why the area became known as 'the Black Country'.

no longer supply coal in sufficient quantities, shafts and tunnels were sunk to exploit thicker and richer layers underground. In this way coalmining as we know it was introduced and the first colliery towns came into existence.

Perhaps the most important invention of all came in 1765 when James Watt finally perfected a steam engine which was both easy to use and economical to run. This entirely revolutionized all concepts of power and put British industry more than a generation ahead of its European competitors.

The coming of machinery and especially the advent of steam power opened up a new world. Between 1700 and 1800 coal output rose from 2½ million to 10 million tons, and by 1830 had reached 25 million tons. The production of pig iron increased at an equally astounding rate: from 30,000 tons in 1750 to 250,000 tons in 1800. In other ways too Britain was changing. New methods of transport, the canals and later the railways, were developed, while around the coast ever larger sailing ships were being built to carry the increasing loads. As we shall see, such changes led to the most rapid town expansion yet experienced.

Mines, Factories and Mills

The mines, factories and mills which suddenly sprang up all over the country were the archetypal products of the Industrial Revolutiom, and it was around these that Britain's industrial towns developed.

The coming of machines to British industry meant its complete transformation. In all types of manufacturing the old methods of production were going out of use. No more was cloth, ironware and pottery made by hand in people's own cottages. Machines had taken over. These were much faster and produced goods much more cheaply than ever people had done, but they were also very large, very cumbersome and very expensive to instal. Only wealthy merchants and industrialists could afford to use them, and only large, specially designed buildings could house them. Thus industries became centralized and were concentrated in factories and mills.

Factories and mills were built wherever there was a source of power or some other natural advantage. Mostly they appeared on coalfields where the new mines were able to supply ever increasing amounts of coal and coke for iron smelting and for steam power. Where imported raw materials were used, however, as with the cotton industry, the ports saw most of the expansion.

In this way Britain's great industrial regions came into being. Coalmining flourished in South Wales, the Clyde Valley in Scotland, in Yorkshire and Derbyshire, and in Northumberland. Lancashire became the principal cotton producing area, while across the Pennines the woollen industry centred on Bradford and Leeds. In Sheffield the iron and steel industry was particularly successful, and at Stoke-on-Trent several great pottery factories were built — to the extent that the whole area became known as 'The Potteries'.

To these new mines, factories and mills flocked thousands of people. The Agricultural Revolution had done much to accelerate the movement of population away from the countryside to the towns. As machines took over so more farm workers were laid off. Neither was the lot of their wives any better since the new textile mills and machinery meant that they could no longer earn a little money by spinning and weaving at home. There was nothing for these poor families to do but move to where there was at least a hope of employment. The mines, factories and mills offered this hope.

Thus vast towns grew up around their industrial core. In many places this happened almost overnight. Villages and hamlets were suddenly transformed into large sprawling towns, and areas that had quite recently been countryside quickly became covered with densely packed houses. Examples of such growth are abundant. In 1750 Bolton was 'a single rough and ill-paved street with thatched cottages'; by the end of the century it had a population of 17,000. During the same period Oldham grew from a village of 300 inhabitants to a town of 12,000. The expansion of the large cities was equally dramatic. In 1700 Manchester had less than 10,000 people; by 1800 it was Britain's largest town outside London with 95,000 inhabitants, and by 1820 this figure had risen to 150,000. In just 30 years, between 1800 and 1830, Birmingham, Sheffield, Liverpool, Leeds, Glasgow and Edinburgh all more than doubled in size. By 1830 half the population of the entire country — some 8 million people — lived in towns. Britain had been transformed into an industrialized and urbanized nation.

32 Samuel Crompton, 1753-1827.

56 Canals

Another reason for the great expansion of towns during the Industrial Revolution was the coming of canals. Even with the improvements brought about by the turnpike system and the progress made in building road surfaces by men such as John Metcalfe and Thomas Telford, overland transport remained difficult throughout the eighteenth century. This was never more true than for goods' traffic. Journeys by stage waggon — the equivalent of our modern lorries — were very slow, very costly and not always reliable. Thus for a long time water transport remained the easiest, cheapest and most efficient way of moving heavy or bulky goods around the country. There was much inter-coastal traffic along Britain's coastline, and all the major navigable rivers, like the Thames, Severn and Trent, were in constant use. But with British industries expanding at such a tremendous rate, the existing waterways were soon insufficient. To relieve them, new, man-made waterways had to be constructed.

The first successful canal was completed in 1776. Financed by the Duke of Bridgewater and planned by James Brindley, it ran from Manchester to Runcorn on the River Mersey, a distance of 56 kms. This was soon followed by an even more ambitious scheme: the digging of a canal to link the River Mersey with the River Trent 149 kms away. But the Great Trunk Canal, as it was called, was only the first in a whole network of artificial waterways cutting across the Midlands and north of England. The Canal Age had begun. Everywhere new schemes were being planned and new projects undertaken. Vast sums of money were invested by landowners eager for a quick return, and men who discovered a flair for surveying or engineering could shoot to fame as canal builders. Such was this 'canal mania' that by the turn of the century every major town was served by a canal, and many places inland and formerly of little importance had grown into busy ports. Birmingham above all became the 'canal metropolis' of Britain and acquired a flourishing export trade. As a result of this the town's growth was rapid: during the first 30 years of the nineteenth century its population rose from 71,000 to 144,000. Other canal towns experienced similar expansion. In the same period Stoke-on-Trent grew from 23,000 to 52,000 inhabitants, and Leicester from 17,000 to 41,000.

Sometimes the presence of a canal was enough to cause a whole new town to be built from scratch. Selby, for example, grew from almost nothing at the point where the Ferrybridge Canal joined the River Ouse. A similar phenomenon occurred at Goole, where, in just 20 years, the Air-Calder Canal Company transformed a relatively small village into a town many thousands strong.

By 1830 Britain had over 4,000 miles of canals. The Canal Age had done much to expand British industry and had produced untold wealth for the new manufacturing towns. Who would have guessed that canal building was about to reach an abrupt end?

33 New coalpits opened up all over the country. This one is near Broseley in Shropshire.

34 Canals became the main thoroughfares for Britain's trade. This canal, at Bath, served the great port of Bristol.

The reason for the sudden end of canals was the arrival of a new form of transport: the railways. Steam-powered trains had been in existence since the beginning of the century, but it was not until the 1830s that railways really came into their own. As early as 1804 Richard Trevithick had invented a small steam locomotive which was capable of running on rails at 16 kms an hour. This was the first of its kind and was primarily designed to be used in coalmines for bringing the coal out from the tunnels. Unfortunately lack of money meant that little further work was done on this locomotive, and another ten years elapsed before George Stephenson developed an improved version of the machine. The success of this locomotive led to more advances, and in 1825 the first public railway was opened between Stockton and Darlington. Soon 'railway mania' was gripping the country to an even greater extent than 'canal mania' had done a generation earlier. In 1830 there were just 111 kms of track; by 1843 there were 3,200 kms, and in 1870 there were as many as 25,000 kms.

Unfortunately there was no attempt to plan a proper railway network of the kind we have today. Parliament allowed the establishment of various independent companies, and this resulted in the frequent duplication of lines, with more than one company building along exactly the same route. Nevertheless, progress was rapid. By 1845 London was linked by rail to Dover, Brighton, Southampton, Bristol, Birmingham, Lancaster and York.

These new railways had far-reaching effects on the development of towns, perhaps the most noticeable of which was the spread of suburbs. Railway stations were usually built on the edge of town, partly for amenity reasons, since the noise and smoke of trains were considered unpleasant, and partly because a great deal of open land was needed for tracks, platforms and sheds. Very quickly, however, people began to realize that the fast and easy transport provided by the railways meant that they could now live on the edge of town, in the cleaner, more healthy atmosphere, and travel to and from work by train. In this way suburbs developed along all the main railway lines, and the railway stations were swallowed up in the towns.

This development occurred in most of Britain's important towns: at Exeter, for example, and at Bristol, at York and at Oxford. But it was in London that this suburban growth was most marked. Each individual railway company built its own station on the capital's outskirts: at Paddington, Euston, King's Cross, Victoria and Waterloo, and these soon became part of the general urban area. Further out, along the railway lines leading out of London, new suburbs also appeared. It was at about this time — towards the middle of the nineteenth century — that areas like Hampstead, Finsbury Park, Stoke Newington and Leytonstone were built.

In some parts of the country the effect of the railways was even more dramatic. Where lines converged at large junctions, or where shunting and repair sheds were built, whole new towns developed from nothing. The growth of these new railway towns, like Swindon, Eastleigh and Crewe, was as sudden as that of the industrial towns had been in the north. This can best be seen at Crewe where, between 1843 and 1870, the population rose from a mere 203 to 18,000. A staggering increase by any standards!

These new railway towns, like the canal towns and industrial towns, were unlike anything ever known before. Previously the growth of urban centres had been gradual, taking place over a thousand years of history. Now, suddenly, vast towns had appeared as if by magic. Their houses, factories and mills were creeping ever outward into the green fields, submerging everything along their path.

35 Some of the early railways.

36 The opening of the Glasgow and Garnkirk Railway, 1831.

Chapter 6
Victorian Towns

Housing Conditions

It is not hard to imagine what these industrial towns were like a hundred years ago. Many of them still exist in northern England, in South Wales and central Scotland: smoky, dismal, dirty places spreading out in all directions for miles on end. There are no public parks and only a few trees dotted here and there break the monotony of the grey buildings. The only open spaces are areas of wasteland where houses have been demolished or where factories store their rubbish. In the mining areas there is even greater ugliness with mountains of coal-slag towering over the rooftops and the old mine workings disused and deserted. These are the typical industrial towns.

In the nineteenth century there were no planning controls or local authority building restrictions as there are today. Houses were therefore built anywhere and everywhere on whatever land happened to be available. This usually meant that, while the steep slopes were avoided, areas of flat land, and especially valleys, quickly became crammed with buildings. The lack of planning controls meant that houses were frequently put up next to or even adjoining the factories and mills. Apart from the town centres themselves, there were few shopping districts. Instead, small grocery and general stores were dotted around the residential areas, usually as local 'corner shops', to supply the daily needs of the inhabitants.

Since all land was owned either by the gentry or by wealthy industrialists all development depended on them. But while some were quick to sell their land to building firms, others were not. This often led to some strange irregularities. For example, areas of densely packed houses and factories might be found next to open farmland with just a fence or road to divide them. In other places streets might come to an abrupt end as they reached a land boundary, or houses might be foreshortened in order to squeeze into a limited building plot at the edge of a particular area.

Indeed, so great was the speed of development that aspects of the countryside were often incorporated into the towns. Old stone walls which once divided fields might survive between gardens, and farmhouses were frequently found alongside modern terraces. Even public footpaths were

37 This picture of Durham underlines the difference between the irregular pattern of the old city and the neat rows of Victorian terraces built to house workmen and their families.

maintained. In Yorkshire, it is still possible to find houses with narrow passages or 'snickets' running right through them where even today people have the right to walk. In one part of Bradford a single footpath wends its way, through snickets, across no less than 16 rows of houses!

The houses built in these industrial towns were not of course all identical. They varied greatly both in size and style depending on the wealth of the people expected to live in them.

The dwellings built and owned by the middle classes — the mill and factory owners and professional people like doctors, lawyers and accountants — were quite good. Usually sited on the edge of town, they were fairly large and were often built in the new mock Gothic style of architecture. This was a very grand style with towers, turrets and gables which made buildings appear much older than they really were. These houses might have as many as four or five bedrooms, a dining room, a pantry and a parlour, a lavatory with flushing water and a bathroom. They even had rooms in the basement for servants. An average middle-class family could usually afford to employ at least two domestics: a cook and a housemaid, and possibly also a butler and a gardener.

The dwellings intended for poorer people, however, were not as pleasant. They were usually built in long rows, and were erected as quickly and as cheaply as possible. Only the cheapest and shoddiest materials were used in their construction, and only the meanest facilities were provided, sometimes not even running water. They had little or no garden and the front door generally opened straight out onto the pavement.

The houses were also extremely tiny. Every scrap of land was used by the profit-hungry developers who aimed to build as many homes as possible on any given piece of ground. Thus, row upon row of small terraces sprang up, each house having only two or three rooms. Upstairs one bedroom was provided for the whole family — often with as many as 10 or 12 children — and downstairs there was a kitchen and a parlour. This economy made it possible to jam up to 127 houses into a single acre, and so brought rich profits to the developers.

In some towns densities were even higher. In Lancashire, for example, tenement blocks became common. Houses were built six or seven storeys high and each floor was let out as a separate dwelling, rather like our modern blocks of flats. In Yorkshire, back-to-back terraces were more usual. These had a dividing wall running down the centre and front doors along each side. The houses were often only 3 or 4 metres wide, and since they backed directly onto another dwelling, there was no through ventilation. Windows were only possible on one side, the front.

So tiny and shoddily-built were these houses that many soon deteriorated into the worst slums Britain had known. In the absence of planning controls the sanitary arrangements were frequently almost non-existent. Toilets were not provided for each individual house but were placed outside, in a courtyard, so that one would serve maybe a whole terrace. And the toilets themselves were primitive in the extreme: a wooden or tin shed built around a simple hole in the earth. Only occasionally would the hole be emptied and then it meant that the sewage had to be carried away in buckets right through the house.

Even towards the end of the nineteenth century, after some improvements had taken place, many dreadful slums still survived. In 1883 George Sims wrote a book, *The Bitter Cry of Outcast London*, in which he described in detail some of the dwellings in the capital:

> To get into them you have to penetrate courts reeking with poisonous and malodorous gases arising from accumulations of sewage and refuse scattered in all directions and often flowing beneath your feet; courts many of them which the sun never penetrates, which are never visited by a breath of fresh air, and which rarely know the virtues of a drop of cleansing water . . . You have to grope your way along dark and filthy passages swarming with vermin

38 In the streets conditions resembled those of Tudor times. This engraving shows nineteenth-century Cowgate in Edinburgh.

. . . Walls and ceilings are black with the accretions of filth which have gathered upon them through long years of neglect. It is exuding through cracks in the boards overhead; it is running down the walls; it is everywhere. What goes by the name of a window is half of it stuffed with rags or covered by boards . . . As to furniture — you may perchance discover a broken chair, the tottering relics of an old bedstead, or the mere fragment of a table; but more commonly you will find rude substitutes for these things in the shape of rough boards resting upon bricks, an old hamper or box turned upside down, or more frequently still, nothing but rubbish and rags.

But it was not just inside the houses that was damp, dark, foul-smelling and rat-infested. Outside, too, the streets were narrow, unpaved and full of holes; sewage overflowed from the drains; there was no collection of refuse, and drinking water was sometimes so scarce that it had to be bought from street traders.

39 'I'll punch your 'ead, directly, if you don't leave orff. How do yer think the What's-a-names 'll bite, if you keep on a splashin' like that!' The humour of this *Punch* cartoon of 1854 does not make the poverty any less real.

In such conditions epidemic diseases flourished. In particular, cholera and typhoid frequently swept through the towns, killing as much as half the population in many areas. One child in every three born in an industrial district died before it reached the age of five.

As the population rose, so overcrowding in the towns became ever more acute. Millions of families began to rent, not houses, but single rooms, and even then were forced, through lack of money, to share with others. The tenements and terraces alike became so congested that even their waterlogged cellars were let out as separate dwellings. In each room, perhaps only 2.5 metres square, there might be as many as five people living cramped together.

Conditions at Work

The conditions for the poor at work were even worse than their homes. Most factory-, mill- and mine-owners had only one aim: to expand production and increase their profits. As a result they cared little about the needs or indeed the welfare of their unfortunate employees.

The working day was long, hard and often dangerous. Adults, both men and women, worked anything from 12 to 18 hours each day, and even young children for up to 10 hours. In the stuffy, unventilated factories and mills the parents operated machines and stoked furnaces while their children turned handles and crawled under machinery to pick fluff off the floor. Conditions in the coalmines were even harsher. As the men worked at the coalface women and children had to drag trucks of coal through the dark, flooded tunnels to the surface. At one Scottish mine they were forced to carry coal-baskets up a series of ladders for a distance equal to the height of St Paul's Cathedral. Their hours of work were so long that some mineworkers did not see the light of day for weeks on end. They would leave home before dawn, work all day underground and finish after sunset. Even Sundays were liable to be taken up in overtime or as part of shift work.

Wages were low, varying usually between 10 and 30 shillings (50p — £1.50) a week. Consequently few people could afford to eat more than just dry bread with, perhaps, a small lump of cheese or meat once or twice a week. At one mill a number of apprentices were discovered fighting with the pigs in the yard in order to take the swill left in the troughs. In some places breaks during the working day for rest and refreshment were almost non-existent. One report stated: 'breakfast a quarter of an hour, and dinner half an hour, and drinking a quarter of an hour'; and this was by no means uncommon for an 18-hour day. Moreover, often even these short breaks were taken up by extra work since all employees were expected to keep their machines clean, and this had to be done outside normal working hours.

Yet despite the terrible conditions, jobs in the factories and mines were much sought after. This was because the alternatives were far worse. Those without regular employment had to earn money as best they could. Some

66 became street traders, selling anything from matches and shoelaces to secondhand clothes. Others did odd jobs like sharpening knives and mending shoes. Yet others became buskers and collected coppers by singing or playing instruments along the streets. Women who were unmarried and out of work found life even more difficult, and many were forced into crime or even prostitution, as the only means of keeping body and soul together.

Those who were neither costers nor buskers nor beggars suffered an even worse fate in the institutions of the time. In the workhouses, hospitals and lunatic asylums sanitary arrangements were foul, food consisted usually of thin gruel, and cruelty was common. Lunatics, for example, were kept in dark, damp, overcrowded cells, and were sometimes stripped naked, chained to the walls and whipped by warders who were often more insane than they were. Not surprisingly few who entered such places ever came out alive.

40 At work in the British Needle Mills, Redditch.

41 Child labour in the mines. These children were called 'putters' or 'trolley boys'.

42 Lodging-houses provided temporary homes for the poor. This one, in St Giles's, London, was for women only. The owners of such places charged 3d or 4d a night and frequently became rich on the profits they made.

Despite the appalling conditions suffered at home and at work, the poorer classes who lived in the industrial towns of the nineteenth century were probably better off than ever before. They were definitely better off than those who remained in the country and worked on the farms. They ate more meat, vegetables and bread — though this was still very little — and stood a better chance of reaching a ripe old age. Indeed, during the reign of Queen Victoria (1837-1901) the lives of the working classes were more healthy, more interesting and more varied than they had been under any previous monarch.

There were, for example, many more facilities provided. More people could read and write and newspapers had become cheap enough for even the less well-off to buy. The postal service improved with the introduction of Rowland Hill's penny post in 1840, and friendly societies like the Ancient Order of Foresters and Hearts of Oak were set up to help the working classes insure themselves against sickness and unemployment. Thrift was encouraged, and the Post Office Savings Bank, founded in 1861, allowed greater numbers to save part of their wages without fear that their money would simply disappear.

Transport was also more readily available. The upper classes still possessed their own private carriages, but for short journeys through town they might hire a hansom cab or a brougham. These were horse-drawn vehicles and were used in much the same way as our modern taxi-cabs. For the poorer classes there was a system of public transport. In 1829 the first horse-drawn omnibus was introduced. This had seats both upstairs and downstairs, and was capable of carrying over 40 passengers. Later, as an alternative to the 'buses, trams were developed. These also were horse-drawn but, unlike their competitors, they ran along rails down the middle of the street. Since both types of vehicle carried large numbers of people, fares were kept low so that even the poor could afford to use them.

But where did people travel to in these new machines? On weekdays it was probably to work; in the evenings and on Saturdays it was possibly to a public house or to visit friends, but on Sundays it was almost certainly to church.

By the Victorian era religion had once again become an important force in people's lives, and churchgoing had risen to a popularity unknown since the Middle Ages. Every Sunday whole families dressed up in their best clothes and went once, twice, three times to church. Congregations became much larger and in all the industrial towns new churches were built to meet the growing demand. Like the houses of the middle classes, these churches were designed in the mock Gothic style. By using stained-glass windows, turrets, spires and buttresses, the builders aimed to recreate the great cathedrals of the past, often with some success. Victorian churches have been criticised for their architecture, but there is little doubt that they did much to improve and add interest to the naturally dull and drab appearance of our major towns.

This period also saw the establishment of the summer holiday as an annual

event. The new railways meant that nowhere in Britain was very far from the 69
coast, and yearly visits to the seaside were soon being made by rich and poor
alike. The resorts of the eighteenth century were given a new lease of life, and
elsewhere new holiday centres developed like Blackpool, Minehead, Torquay,
Margate and Southend. Hotels and guest houses sprang up, piers and
promenades were built, and there were even such modern amusements as boat
trips, donkey rides and penny slot machines. For many working people, their
annual holiday was the only break in an otherwise hard life.

43 Victorian Gothic architecture: Truro Cathedral, begun in 1880. The only medieval part
of the building is the south aisle, seen in the foreground.

44 Seaside resorts suddenly expanded. This photograph shows Ventnor, Isle of Wight, in 1898.

The Philanthropists

The dreadful living conditions of the poor did not go entirely unnoticed. From the earliest days of the Industrial Revolution there had been people who cared for the working classes and who worked hard to improve their lot. It was these philanthropists who were largely responsible for the first real improvements in towns and town life.

At the beginning of the nineteenth century, Elizabeth Fry did much to ease prison conditions and to extend education. William Cobbett, in his writings and speeches, brought to public notice the plight of the poor in the northern slums and, by doing this, caused certain reforms to be made in the distribution of alms to the needy. A contemporary of his, Robert Owen, was another philanthropist. It was he who pioneered improvements in factory conditions and, by the example of his own mills in New Lanark near Glasgow, showed how a more generous attitude towards employees could actually increase production. By the start of Queen Victoria's reign in 1837 philanthropists had gained considerable influence and public support. During the next 40 years they were to gain, in addition, a certain degree of political power.

The two most prominent philanthropists of the Victorian era were Lord Shaftesbury and Sir Edwin Chadwick. Lord Shaftesbury was chiefly concerned with working conditions and especially with the treatment of women and children in factories. Unlike previous social reformers he was a Member of Parliament and was therefore in a better position to influence government action. In 1833 he had already helped to pass a Factory Act which stopped all textile factories from employing children under 9 years of age, and reduced the hours of work for children between the ages of 9 and 18. But this was only the first in a long line of reforms for which he was responsible. In 1842 the Mines Act banned all women and children under 10 from working underground, and two years later a second Factory Act reduced the hours of work for women and made further reductions in the hours worked by children. In 1847 and 1850 the conditions in textile factories were again improved, and in 1860, 1861 and 1864 more acts were passed to bring other places, notably bleaching and dyeing factories and potteries, under stricter control. Lord Shaftesbury was also active in other fields, and before he died in 1885 his work had improved conditions in lunatic asylums, banned the use of climbing boys, and established a system of schooling for poor children.

45 Workmen's houses designed by Prince Albert and exhibited at the Great Exhibition of 1851.

While Lord Shaftesbury concentrated on working conditions, Edwin Chadwick turned his attention to conditions in people's homes. He sat on various government committees and in his role as adviser did much to help formulate an official policy of social reform. The Public Health Act of 1848, for example, was largely his work. This set up a Board of Health and laid down certain laws governing the sanitary arrangements in towns. Other similar reforms followed, and when he died Chadwick left part of his fortune in trust for the promotion of sanitary science.

But it was not only individuals working by themselves or with small groups of friends who wanted to help the poor. There were also large organizations devoted to philanthropic work. Perhaps the most famous was the Salvation Army, which was founded by 'General' Booth with the aim of converting to Christianity all social outcasts such as the homeless, the hungry and the petty criminal. The Salvation Army built missions — or 'citadels' as they were and still are called — and from these administered its social work. Tramps were provided with food and shelter, the sick were given medical treatment, and the unemployed, if possible, were found jobs.

Another philanthropic organization was Total Abstinence, a group set up to fight the evils of alcohol. The situation had improved little since the eighteenth century, and drunkenness was still a great social scourge. It was partly due to the efforts of this group that, in the end, the government strengthened the licensing laws, and limited opening hours in public houses.

The reforms we have mentioned so far, even when instigated by Act of Parliament, resulted from individual, isolated demands for urban improvements. They were not part of a concerted general policy. However, as the nineteenth century progressed the government accepted increasing responsibility for the conditions in towns, and in many ways took over from the philanthropists in the fight against poor social standards.

The first step in this direction came in 1829 when Sir Robert Peel, the Home Secretary, set up London's Metropolitan Police Force — the first of its kind in Britain. Its success soon led to the establishment of similar forces in many parts of the country and this in turn reduced the crime rate and made towns safer places in which to live.

In 1835 came the most significant reform of all since it was to lead directly to all further town improvements: the Municipal Corporations Act. This made provision for every town to be governed by a borough council, which would be responsible for administering its own urban area and organizing such new services as refuse collection, fire prevention, public libraries, baths and education. Street lighting was also improved. The old tin bowls of whale-oil and cotton wicks which had passed for street illumination for so long were replaced by gaslight. By 1855, this had been installed in every major British town.

To encourage town improvements still further the government provided grants for local authorities who wished to undertake new schemes, and appointed inspectors to check that official standards were maintained. In 1875 a second Public Health Act was passed which was more effective than Chadwick's 1848 Act. It strengthened the powers of the Board of Health and established a nationwide system of sanitary authorities under the control of the Board of Health, to supervise all aspects of sanitation in towns. In the same year the Artisans' Dwellings Act gave councils the power to demolish whole areas of slums and rebuild from scratch.

Nowhere were town improvements as fast nor as successful as in Birmingham. Within a few years the city was transformed from a typical industrial black-spot to one of the most advanced towns in Britain. This achievement was due almost entirely to the work of just one man, Joseph Chamberlain, who, as the town's mayor, used to the full the powers given him by the government. In one particular scheme an area of over 40 acres was cleared, and in place of the old slums there arose a new estate of houses, a public park and a shopping centre. Between 1873 and 1876 Birmingham, in Chamberlain's words, was 'parked, paved, assized, marketed, gas and watered and improved'.

Naturally, where Birmingham led, other towns followed. By the end of the century every town had acquired the basic standards of good sanitation: clean streets, efficient drains and piped running water.

46 (*Left*) Bow Street, London, in the late 1830s. The police (on the left) were nicknamed alternately 'Peelers', 'Roberts' and 'Bobbies' after their founder. Notice also the newly paved road and the gas lighting.

74 Improvements in Transport

Urban transport, too, was improving fast. In 1863 the world's first underground railway was opened in London. The line ran for just 6½ kms from Paddington Station to Farringdon Street, and was built only just under the surface. Nevertheless, short as it was, it marked the beginning of a new era in town communications. Soon the rest of the present Metropolitan Line was completed and work had begun on others. In 1890 London's first deep 'tube' was opened, the City and South London Railway, and ten years later came the first electrified line: from the Bank to Shepherd's Bush (part of the modern Central Line). By the end of Queen Victoria's reign in 1901, the London underground railway system reached as far as Hampstead, Finsbury Park and Clapham.

At that time only two other British cities provided an alternative to surface transport: Liverpool had an overhead electric railway built on viaducts, and Glasgow had tube trains operated by cable haulage. London's system was the most advanced and was soon copied all over the world — notably in Moscow, New York and Paris.

The coming of electricity did not only help underground transport. It also made surface travelling much quicker. Soon every tramway in the country was electrified. Leeds was first to change in 1891, then came Bristol in 1895, Glasgow, Hull and Liverpool in 1898, and London at the turn of the century.

By the end of the nineteenth century therefore, the worst horrors of the Industrial Revolution were over, although many slums remained to be cleared. To a large extent British towns had already grown into what they are today. There remained, however, one innovation which was to have a major effect on their appearance — the coming of the motor car.

47 (*Opposite top*) Bradford Town Hall, 1886. 'Civic pride' led to the erection of some magnificent municipal buildings.

48 (*Opposite*) Liverpool in 1891. A town before the motor car.

Chapter 7
The Twentieth Century

The Motor Age

In 1887 the first light-engined motor car was introduced by Gottlieb Daimler, a German inventor and engineer. Eight years later, in 1895, the first motor exhibition was held in London, and the following summer a motor car made its first appearance in the Lord Mayor's Show. Few people then could have foreseen that, within a mere half-century, this new method of transport would have transformed British towns for all time.

By the start of the First World War in 1914, the internal combustion engine was already beginning to compete with both horse-drawn carriages and the railways. In many towns petrol-driven omnibuses had replaced their slower predecessors, and private motor cars were being built in ever increasing numbers. Road surfaces were improved and various Acts of Parliament allowed for ever faster speeds. At the end of the Second World War in 1945 there were 2 million cars in private ownership in Britain; by 1957 this figure had doubled. Today it is estimated that there may be as many as 20 million cars on British roads.

The effects of the motor car have been numerous and far-reaching. Most important of all, it has allowed the residential areas in towns to be divided from industrial areas. People no longer had to live within easy walking distance or within a short train- or tram-ride from their place of work. Instead they could live well away from the factories (where noise, dirt and smells often made life unpleasant) and commute daily by car or motor-bus. The character of towns changed. Houses were built in groups in residential areas, and industries developed on large trading estates or colonies.

The coming of motor transport also encouraged the rapid spread of suburbs. The population of Britain was still growing fast, from 37 million in 1901 to 46 million by 1921. And this increase had to be almost entirely accommodated in the towns since new methods of agriculture meant that less and less workers were needed on the land. Towns, then, expanded ever outward to house the growing population, and new suburbs spread out in all directions from the city centre. Most of these suburbs are not unpleasant areas: groups of little houses set back from the road and surrounded by a small garden. Each house is usually

49 (*Left*) In 1908 London Transport used this poster to advertise its underground system. Such has been town expansion that nobody would think of depicting Golders Green like this today.

50 (*Below*) An early motor car. The Lanchester of 1908.

either semi-detached or in a block of three or four, with two or three bedrooms, two living rooms, a kitchen and a bathroom. Many soon acquired a garage as car ownership became increasingly common — even for the less well-off. Unfortunately, the growing importance of motor transport meant that many of these suburbs became ribbon developments, extending out from the town in narrow bands along the main roads, leaving only the wedges of farmland between unspoilt.

As suburbs sprawled across the countryside so the small outlying towns and villages were swallowed up and lost their identity. The large cities began to incorporate neighbouring settlements, so that in the end the built-up areas covered vast expanses. Conurbations were the result: immense urban regions enveloping several formerly separate towns. Greater London, for example, now stretches for more than 30 kms across and has a population of over 10 million people.

52 (*Opposite top*) View across Edgware, 1930.

53 (*Opposite bottom*) The same view in 1957. Modern houses and roads have been built to join Edgware with the rest of Greater London.

51 (*Below*) A typical suburb built between the two World Wars: Camberley in Surrey.

Garden Cities

Town expansion, however, did not always follow the same pattern or share the same characteristics. The horrors of the industrial towns, with their crowded, dirty houses and streets, led many people to look for 'ideal' towns where the benefits of an urban environment could be combined with the pleasures of the countryside: trees, parks, fresh air and so on. The result was the building first of Garden Suburbs and later of Garden Cities.

The first Garden Suburb was started as early as 1875, when the building of Bedford Park in west London included the planting of hundreds of trees and the provision for large areas of playing fields. However, it was not until the beginning of the twentieth century that the idea really took on. In 1907 work began on one of the most famous of all these developments, Hampstead Garden Suburb in north London. Here the houses were built at a low density — only eight to the acre — and in all styles and sizes so that the area would attract different classes of people, from the very rich to the very poor.

The success of the Garden Suburbs encouraged planners to design whole towns on the same principle. In this respect the work of Ebenezer Howard is particularly important, and it was largely due to his efforts that the first ever Garden City, at Letchworth in Hertfordshire, was begun in 1903. Later, in 1919, a second Garden City was built at Welwyn, also in Hertfordshire. Both became thriving towns and laid the foundations for much future town planning.

However, successful as they were, schemes such as the new Garden Cities could not solve the enormous problems being faced by many British towns. Despite the reforms introduced in the nineteenth century, there was still no comprehensive system of control over urban development and the location of industries. As the country's population continued to expand, the growth of suburbs and the increase in car ownership were in danger of destroying all that was good in town life.

In 1937, therefore, a Royal Commission was set up under Sir Montague Barlow to consider ways of improving urban conditions. The resulting Barlow Report, published in 1940, concluded:

> The disadvantages in many, if not in most, of the great industrial concentrations, alike on the strategical, the social and the economic side, do constitute serious handicaps and even in some respects dangers to the nation's life and development, and we are of the opinion that definite action should be taken by government toward remedying them.

With its proposal that the government should take on wide-ranging powers to deal with all aspects of town development, the Barlow Report marked a landmark in the history of British towns. It led directly to the Town and Country Planning Act of 1947, which brought into being the Ministry of Town and Country Planning — later to be called the Ministry of Housing and Local Government — and directed all future government planning policy.

The effects were far-reaching indeed. From now on all development plans, both industrial and residential, had to be approved by the government before work could begin. This did much to stop ugly and substandard buildings from being erected; it also helped to limit the untidy spread of urban areas.

The havoc wrought by enemy bombers during the Second World War (1939-45) gave the government a further opportunity to rebuild many towns. Under the direction of the Ministry of Housing and Local Government grants were provided for the construction of new roads, new schools and new hospitals; all over the country new factories and houses sprang up, well planned and specially located to improve working and living conditions.

At the same time the government introduced a programme of council-house building in order to provide homes at low rents for those who would otherwise be homeless or living in substandard accommodation. Between 1950 and 1955 nearly 1½ million council houses were built in England and Wales alone. The number has continued to rise so that today every town has its council estate; unfortunately, as a result of the need for economy, this is only too often a monotonous area in which all the houses are small, drab and seemingly identical.

54 (*Left*) Rural shades in a Garden City: Meadow Way, Letchworth.

Since the late 1950s the government has taken even wider powers with its regional policy, which aims to disperse both industries and population more evenly over the country. To relieve overcrowding, people and firms are being encouraged to move out of the larger towns and settle in smaller towns where there is more room to build, and economic help is being given to regions with declining industries or a falling population.

New Towns

In some areas, in order to accommodate the overspill population from the large industrial centres, the government has actually built completely new towns.

In 1946 the New Towns Act made provision for the building of 14 new urban settlements in Britain. Each was to be entirely self-contained, with its own industries, schools, shopping centres and so on, and the houses were planned in pleasant and quiet surroundings. It was also hoped that the New Towns would achieve a social and economic balance. The Final Report of the New Towns Committee stated:

> Businesses and industries established should include not only factories, shops, and the businesses and services meeting local needs, but head-offices and administrative and research establishments including sections of government departments and other public offices.

The first New Towns included Stevenage, Crawley, Harlow, Hatfield and Basildon. In many ways their design was revolutionary. Roads, for example, were graded and built with special attention to the surroundings: those constructed to take through-traffic were made wide and built round the edge of the town, away from the residential areas, while those planned for local traffic were narrower and set in strict patterns to give easy access to both homes and shops. The residential areas were located deliberately away from the industrial buildings in order to make people's lives quieter, safer and more healthy.

So successful were these first New Towns that more recently others have been built, like Cumbernauld in Scotland, and even today further New Towns are being planned: Washington on Tyneside, Runcorn in Lancashire and Milton Keynes in Buckinghamshire are three such schemes. We shall have to wait a few more years before we know whether these, too, are going to be successful.

55 (*Opposite top*) Canterbury after an air-raid during the Second World War. Bombing partly destroyed many of our oldest towns.

56 (*Opposite*) A council house estate in the 1950s: Leicester.

84   Green Belts and Government Controls

At the same time as building new urban areas, the government is also helping to save a great deal of what is good from the past.

In order to stop the continual spread of towns into the countryside, the Ministry of Housing and Local Government devised the Green Belt policy. Under this scheme, areas of countryside around large towns are given special protection against house and factory development. Each area is in the shape of a broad ring — perhaps 8 kms wide — around the town. Apart from stopping further urban growth, these Green Belts serve two important functions, by providing town dwellers with attractive countryside in which to walk and take picnics, and by preserving good agricultural land close enough to the town to be of strategic value.

London was the first city to be surrounded by a Green Belt, but was soon followed by others, notably Birmingham, Manchester and Liverpool. There is no doubt that the policy has been successful: much beautiful countryside has remained unspoilt which might otherwise have been lost forever.

Within towns, too, much is being done for preservation. No building can now be demolished without permission, and in the case of attractive or very old buildings, permission is unlikely to be obtained. The authorities also have the power to award preservation orders to places of either historic or architectural interest. Any building protected by a preservation order is usually safe from the ravages of developers.

Other government action is also helping to improve town life. The air pollution caused by smoke and harmful gases is being controlled, and there are now even attempts to limit noise to a certain level. However such attempts at preserving towns and town life are successful only as far as they go. They are generally not sufficient to meet the rapid changes now taking place in our urban   environment.

57 (*Opposite top*) Cumbernauld New Town. Notice the development's regular layout and the way major roads skirt the perimeter of the residential area.

58 (*Opposite*) Greater London. The New Towns have been built along the edge of the Green Belt. Does this mean that London is still spreading outwards?

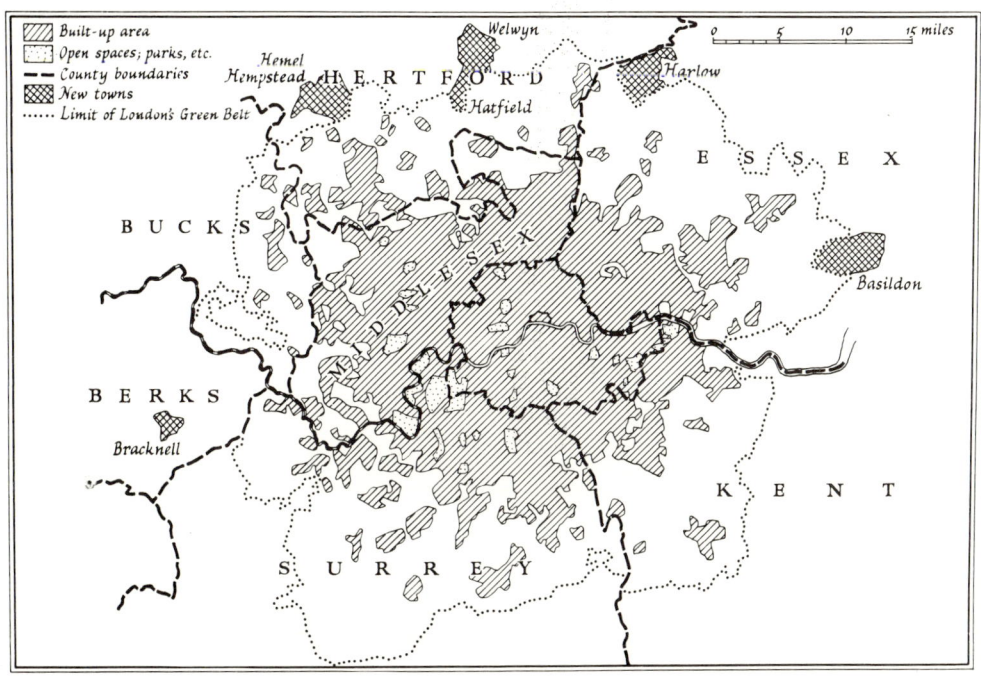

Chapter 8
Towns Today

59 High-rise flats near Sheffield, with Victorian terraces being demolished to make way for modern development.

British towns today are facing possibly their most serious crisis ever. As the population of the country continues to rise — it is at present about 55 million — more and more people want to live in urban areas. The government and local authorities are doing much to maintain standards — of housing, education, transport, welfare — in our towns, but time is running out. Indeed, it is not only living and working conditions in the towns which are in danger of deteriorating, but the very essence of town life itself.

Planning for the Future

One of the most immediate problems is that of town planning. Britain is now passing through a period of change as fundamental as that of the Industrial Revolution two centuries ago. Advances in technology, in particular, are having far-reaching effects on our way of life: on transport, on employment, on leisure and the environment. All this means that planning is becoming more complex. Not only must a greater number of factors, physical and human, be taken into account, but the future is now much harder to forecast than before. It is no longer sufficient for planners to aim at a single and definite goal, whether it be a new road system, a residential development or industrial expansion. Instead they must plan ahead with the knowledge that urban conditions, economic standards and human needs are continually changing; that there can, in fact, be no hard-and-fast decisions on the future of towns.

Until recently town planning was also hindered by the way local government was organized. In large urban areas the system had become complicated and often out of date. This was particularly true of the six main conurbations, London, Leeds, Manchester, Birmingham, Merseyside and Tyneside. Their vast size and the fact that they ran across county boundaries meant that their administration was becoming ever more difficult. In many cases, too, there was a clash between urban and rural interests when one authority controlled areas of town and country and ran such services as sewage, drainage, transport and lighting for both regions.

Now, however, several steps have been taken to rationalize the situation. In 1965 the counties of London and Middlesex were abolished and the 90-odd local councils were combined into 33 new, larger boroughs. It was hoped that these larger administrative regions would be better attuned to modern urban needs, more able to carry out town planning schemes, and more likely to produce greater efficiency and some financial savings. Whether they will or not remains to be seen.

A few years later there was a further attempt to improve urban administration. The Maud Report suggested that England's county boundaries should be redrawn so that the conurbations, instead of being administered by the various county councils into whose areas they extended, should each form their own special metropolitan county. In the case of Leeds, Manchester, Birmingham, Merseyside and Tyneside, this has now been done, although as with the changes in London it is still too soon to judge its success. Nevertheless, such far-reaching schemes at least give hope for better urban planning in the future.

The Housing Problem

Even with improved organization planning is becoming more difficult. The rising population alone is causing problems of overcrowding which seem almost insurmountable. Britain is only a small island and the land available for building is naturally limited. Unless stricter controls on the spread of towns are introduced, there is a real danger that the entire country will be swallowed up in development schemes.

Every day more people need more houses, more factories and more offices. But where can these be built? Certainly much development is continuing on the outskirts of towns but the problems created by this, both in terms of transport and land availability, only heighten the need for redevelopment inside existing urban areas. As a result, over the last 20 years or so, towns have not only grown outwards but upwards. The need to increase the density of houses and offices combined with the availability of steel girders and pre-cast concrete has resulted in the construction of many hundreds of tower blocks. These are both cheap and easy to build, and have now revolutionized the appearance of every one of our towns. In many cases, sadly, they have in the process destroyed some of our finest views. In London, for example, the skyline is no longer dominated by St Paul's Cathedral and the numerous Wren spires which were so much a feature of the eighteenth-century capital. Instead, all one can see is a collection of high, square towers of glass and concrete.

Apart from their ugliness these blocks also have other drawbacks. There is now evidence that they do not, in fact, save space as was originally thought, since so much land is needed around them to provide fresh air, recreation and sunlight. Also recent medical studies would seem to indicate that people living in high-rise flats are often unhappy, unhealthy and even mentally unstable.

The Traffic Problem

The overcrowding of cars in towns is no less of a problem than the overcrowding of people. Even with a rapid road-building programme, roads are becoming increasingly congested. In our historic towns the problem is particularly acute since the old buildings and narrow streets impede traffic movement. Moreover the continual vibration of heavy traffic is damaging the fabric of many old buildings.

Various schemes have been attempted to ease the situation. In some places one-way systems and traffic controls have helped to keep cars on the move and cut down the number of accidents. In other places public transport has been given special priority in the hope of encouraging more people to use it. To this end 'buses only' lanes have been marked out along many urban streets.

Pedestrian precincts, usually in shopping centres, are an attempt to divide road traffic from people on foot and so reduce the number of traffic jams and accidents. Unfortunately this often leads to worse problems being created elsewhere. The motor vehicles banned from pedestrian precincts are forced to use alternative routes through or round a town and this can cause congestion

60 The London skyline today. Only St Paul's Cathedral can compete with the new tower blocks. Compare this with the eighteenth-century view on page 37.

61 A one-way street in the rush hour: Elephant and Castle, London, at 4.45 pm.

where these routes converge. The building of by-passes and urban motorways represent other attempts to ease the problems on the roads but these, like other schemes, have proved only partially successful. Through-traffic can be directed along by-passes to leave town centres quieter and less congested, but their very existence may actually increase the number of vehicles about. When a new road is built there is a tendency for more drivers to use their cars under the impression that traffic conditions will have improved.

Through-traffic is not the only cause of road congestion. When people drive into towns, either to work or to shop, they have to park their cars somewhere and the problem of providing sufficient space for this is a major headache for the planning authorities. In coastal resorts and other holiday towns during the summer the problem is particularly acute. In the 1950s parking meters were introduced as a means of rationing parking facilities. Now, it seems that every inch of spare land has been used up and underground as well as multi-storey car parks have become a common feature of towns and cities. Yet still there are more cars wanting somewhere to park than there are parking spaces available.

The problem appears so intractable that many experts are beginning to think that it has been tackled from the wrong end. They believe that space for cars may attract extra traffic, and so recommend that councils should restrict rather than increase the space available. Indeed, in the future, many local authorities might well ban cars altogether from their urban areas.

Social Problems

The combination of past bad planning, housing problems and traffic congestion has left its mark on the people living in our towns and cities. In fact, in many respects, the resulting social problems are perhaps the most serious of all.

Most of Britain's urban areas are not pleasant places. They are overcrowded and busy, they are dirty and noisy and they are unhealthy. They are also very expensive to live in. Land values in towns have soared in recent years and this has led to great increases in the cost of living. Rents and rates are high, public transport fares are rising, and the price of food, goods and services is generally far above the national average. Consequently both people and firms are now beginning to move out of the towns to cleaner, cheaper and more open suburbs. There is danger in this migration since city centres might lose their importance as focal points and may eventually fall into decline and decay.

In London there is now evidence that this is beginning to take place and that the city centre is gradually dying. In parts of the City itself, and around the main railway stations, large areas are becoming dilapidated and empty. Their populations are leaving, their business premises are closing down, and a blight of stagnation seems finally to have settled over them. The same pattern can be discerned in several other large towns, too.

Another problem which has received a great deal of attention in recent years is the increase in urban violence and delinquency. Overcrowding in certain areas of cities and the effects of high-rise flats on the children brought up in them may be at least partly to blame. Sir Keith Joseph, a Conservative politician, has summed up the present situation like this:

> Some secondary schools in our cities are dominated by gangs operating extortion rackets against small children. Teenage pregnancies are rising; so are drunkenness, sexual offences and crimes of sadism.
>
> For the first time in a century and a half, since the great Tory reformer Robert Peel set up the metropolitan police, areas of our cities are becoming unsafe for peaceful citizens by night, and even some by day.

The arrival of Commonwealth immigrants and their settlement in Britain's major industrial regions have to some extent exacerbated these problems. The immigrants' lack of money and their natural inclination to 'stick to their own kind' have led many of them to crowd together in small, introverted communities, often without proper facilities.

In the years to come social problems of delinquency and overcrowding may well even worsen. But we must not rely only on the government and local authorities to find a solution; we must all play an active part in preserving and improving our urban environment.

62 A pedestrian precinct in Coventry. Here people can do their shopping in safety, away from the noise of traffic.

So fast have been the changes this century in towns and town life that it is unlikely that a person returning to any one of our major cities, even after a gap of just 20 years, would recognize his surroundings. With the accelerating rate of progress, changes are likely to happen even faster in the future.

There has been much speculation about the future shape of towns. Will they remain basically the same, growing gradually upwards and outwards? Or will they alter beyond recognition? One thing is certain — as technology increases its control over our way of life, so computers, newer, faster systems of transport and more complex methods of telecommunication will all have a greater impact on the appearance of our towns and cities.

One view is that people in the future will prefer to stay in their own homes rather than face the polluted and violent outside environment. They would work at home, office workers relying on telephones and manual workers on buttons and dials linked to the centres of production. This would lead to the ultimate death of our cities and the development, instead, of a scatter of isolated buildings all over the country.

Some people, however, take the opposite view. They think that man's natural desire to live in large groups — for protection, friendship and so on — will preserve towns and even perhaps make them more concentrated. Towns might, for example, consist of large towers, each holding thousands of people and rising as much as a kilometre into the sky. The tower would contain everything needed for a town to survive: houses, entertainment, offices and factories. Alternatively great sea-cities might be built on stilts in the shallow waters around the continents and then covered by huge domes of glass or plastic which would maintain an equable climate and a constant atmosphere.

Those still more far-sighted envisage cities held in great space rockets circling the earth or even some cities built on other planets. But none of these forecasts seems particularly attractive to us now. They all suggest that towns in the future will be soulless structures, and our lives in them ordered and controlled entirely by machines. This is obviously an impression — and fear — shared by John Betjeman. In his poem, 'The Planster's Vision', he writes:

> I have a vision of The Future, chum,
> The workers' flats in fields of soya beans
> Tower up like silver pencils, score on score:
> And Surging Millions hear the Challenge come
> From microphones in communal canteens
> 'No Right! No Wrong! All's perfect, evermore'.

If this really does prove to be the nature of towns to come, then it is a sad prospect. But it is not inevitable. Towns, after all, are built by people, and reflect the society for which they are constructed. As long as people continue to appreciate the finer aspects of life and the importance of individual happiness, then we have no need to fear for our towns.

63 The 'Solar Dome': a house designed to be heated entirely by the sun. One day whole towns may be contained within such domes.

64 'Motopia', a vision of the future. This model shows the ground level given over completely to pedestrians while traffic moves freely across the roof-tops.

Further Reading

Books which deal with aspects of towns and town life are too numerous to list. Nearly every general textbook on either geography or history contains information about urban areas. There are, however, more specialized publications and a selection of these is given below.

Books on the History of Towns and Town Life
Gerald Burke, *Towns in the Making* (Edward Arnold, 1971)
D C Money, *Patterns of Settlement* (Evans Bros, 1972)
Peter Moss, *Town Life through the Ages* (Harrap, 1972)
C H B & M Quennell, *Everyday Life in Roman and Anglo-Saxon Times* (Batsford)
C H B & M Quennell, *A History of Everyday Things in England* (Batsford)
C Trent, *Greater London* (Dent, 1965)

Books on Modern Towns and Town Planning
John Haddon, *Local Geography in Towns* (Philip, 1971)
Peter Hall, *London 2000* (Faber, 1963)
E Jones & E Van Zandt, *The City, Yesterday, Today and Tomorrow* (Aldus and Jupiter, 1974)
Michael Palmer, *Cities* (Batsford, 1971)
C B Purdom, *The Letchworth Achievement* (Dent, 1963)
Peter Self, *Cities in Flood* (Faber, 1957)
Tetlow & Goss, *Homes, Towns and Traffic* (Faber, 1965)
Eric Young, *Settlement, Trade and Transport* ('Basic Studies in Geography Series', Edward Arnold, 1973)

Books on British Town Architecture
John Betjeman, *A Pictorial History of English Architecture* (John Murray, 1972)
William Collier, *Historic Buildings* (Spurbooks, 1973)
Nikolaus Pevsner, *The Buildings of England* (Penguin)
M & A Potter, *Houses* (John Murray, 1960)
Roy Worskett, *The Character of Towns* (Architectural Press, 1969)

Wider Study

The above books can, for the most part, either be studied in detail or merely 'dipped into', since they combine interesting and informative texts with clear and useful illustrations. They do not, however, provide the only picture of what towns were like in the past or what they continue to be like. Novels, diaries, biographies, poetry — indeed every form of literature — contain invaluable information about town life. The *Diary of Samuel Pepys*, for example, is a fascinating account of London life at the time of the Great Fire. The novels of Mrs Gaskell, like *Cranford* and *Wives and Daughters,* describe English towns during the Industrial Revolution. Charles Dickens, of course, supplies endless details of the appalling conditions which existed during the Victorian age and cannot be too strongly recommended. On a lighter note, *The Diary of a Nobody* by George and Weedon Grossmith humorously records life in a middle-class London suburb at the end of the last century, while many of John Betjeman's poems do the same for the suburbs of today.

Finally, a word should be said about other ways in which we can find out about towns. Architecture, for example, is an absorbing subject, and it is surprising what can be learned simply by raising our eyes above the level of shop windows and front doors as we walk through our home town. Similarly, a visit to a local museum or even a chat with an elderly person can reveal all sorts of interesting facts about our towns in the past. Today we are largely a nation of town dwellers, and it is only right that we should know and understand something of our environment.

Index

The numbers in **bold** refer to the figure numbers of the illustrations.